A guide to English historical records

A guide to English historical records

ALAN MACFARLANE

6.8.11

To Josh,

wishing you all success
in your thesis from

Alan Macfarlane

CAMBRIDGE UNIVERSITY PRESS

Cambridge
London   New York   New Rochelle
Melbourne   Sydney

CAMBRIDGE UNIVERSITY PRESS
Cambridge, New York, Melbourne, Madrid, Cape Town, Singapore, São Paulo

Cambridge University Press
The Edinburgh Building, Cambridge CB2 8RU, UK

Published in the United States of America by Cambridge University Press, New York

www.cambridge.org
Information on this title: www.cambridge.org/9780521252256

First published 1983
This digitally printed version 2008

A catalogue record for this publication is available from the British Library

Library of Congress Catalogue Card Number: 82-025102

ISBN 978-0-521-25225-6 hardback
ISBN 978-0-521-07980-8 paperback

Contents

Contents

Preface

This short work is intended to complement and extend two earlier
publications. The first of these is a manual on Reconstructing
Historical Communities (1977). In that work we surveyed community
studies in history and social sciences. We described, with
transcripts, twelve major types of document, and then gave a
preliminary inventory of the major sources available to an English
local historian. We set out a method of hand-indexing such
material, with suggestions on how to locate, transcribe and index
it. We assessed in a preliminary way the quality of the data in
relation to a specific source, place, family and individual. We
discussed the use of such material in relation to physical
background, economic life, population studies, social structure,
law, politics, education and religion. Finally we assessed some of
the difficulties and defects of local records: the problems of
record loss, of ambiguities and fictions in the records, the
difficulties of linking together different pieces of information,
of inferring motivation from behaviour, of studying a particular
place given the high degree of mobility and of the invisibility of
certain sections of the population. We concluded by providing some
estimates of the amount of time and energy required to collect and
index the records.

Subsequently we decided to publish full transcripts of all
the records for one English parish up to 1750. With the indexes,
this would have meant a nine-thousand-page publication,

prohibitively costly to produce in ordinary book form. We therefore collaborated with Chadwyck-Healey Ltd in producing a computer-output microfiche edition of the records for a tenth of the price. In order to make the documents comprehensible, we had to spend much time and thought in re-assembling them into archival categories. In order to explain the procedures which produced the printed records and the interconnections of the documents three brief introductory pamphlets were distributed with the microfiche. A number of historians and others who saw the introductions asked for copies, since nothing of this nature existed elsewhere. The present book is essentially a re-publication of what was written as brief introductions to particular sets of documents, plus two further chapters considering the growth in the use of historical documents and other topics. The limitations which the particular history of this book's growth have imposed are discussed in the first two chapters. It should be stressed here that in order to prevent duplication of what was said in Reconstructing Historical Communities and other guides, this introduction does not deal with many of the important questions concerning the reliability and utility of historical documents. Instead, its aim is to provide a single introductory description of how documents were produced and connected to each other. I would have welcomed a guide which provided an overview of record-making institutions and records, but I do not know of any other that attempts in a short space to do this. In order to keep it reasonably priced we have, as before, produced the work using computer-output photo-litho methods. I have also kept the description as brief as possible. Thus, for example, the Webbs devoted two volumes to manor and borough records and another two to the poor law. In this work we have made do with a few pages. Thus the treatment is meant to lead interested readers on to a point where they can consult more exhaustive guides as appropriate.

Acknowledgements

The Social Science Research Council and King's College Research Centre, Cambridge, provided the financial support for investigation of the records described here. Members of the research project, Cherry Bryant, Sarah Harrison, Charles Jardine, Jessica King, Tim King, have all helped to deepen my understanding of the nature of the records. Members of the Department of Social Anthropology and Computing Service at Cambridge and particularly Janet Hall have provided stimulus and support. Professor Geoffrey Elton, Dr Ralph Houlbrooke, Dr Dorothy Owen and Dr Richard Smith have all very kindly read and commented on parts of the text. The last three chapters appeared in a slightly extended form as separate pamphlets to introduce a microfiche edition of Records of an English Village: Earls Colne 1400-1750. This is available from Chadwyck-Healey Ltd, 20 Newmarket Road, Cambridge CB5 8DT, England, who have kindly agreed to allow the material to be re-used. I am grateful to the following institutions and individuals for their kind permission to quote from documents in their possession: the Guildhall Library, London; the Essex Record Office, Chelmsford; the Bishop of London; the vicar and wardens of Earls Colne, Essex; Colonel G.O.C. Probert. Transcription of Crown material in the Public Record Office appears by permission of the Controller of Her Majesty's Stationery Office. The staff of the Essex and Public Record Offices have provided much assistance. My thanks to all of these.

1. Re-discovering the English past

This introduction is designed to help those who wish to re-discover
a world which survived for over five hundred years but is now
rapidly vanishing. We speak of 're-discover' for a number of
changes in the last fifty years are making that world seem strange
and alien, a 'world we have lost' in the title of Peter Laslett's
well-known book (Laslett 1965). This distancing is partly the
result of technological change. As Marc Bloch observed: 'successive
technological revolutions have immeasurably widened the
psychological gap between generations. With some reason, perhaps,
the man of the age of electricity and of the airplane feels himself
far removed from his ancestors' (Bloch 1954:36). Since Bloch wrote,
the pace has quickened and we now have television, computing,
nuclear weapons and a host of other technological gulfs. The
difficulties in understanding are also increasing rapidly as a
result of recent attempts to bring England into the European
community. The measures of weight, distance, length, the principles
and institutions of law and government which were built up over a
thousand years have been or are being rapidly swept away. Old
county boundaries and old communication systems are being changed.
Alongside these changes is a re-shaping of the physical landscape.
During the last thirty years, many of the houses, roads, hedgerows,
woods and fields have been destroyed, old town centres have been
pulled down, ancient landscapes cut in half by motorways.

The difficulties in studying English history over the five

hundred or so years up to 1800 were considerable enough even by the later nineteenth century. Often it was necessary to uncover modes of thought which were almost gone. Thus F.W. Maitland warned that those who would attempt to make a study of the ecclesiastical courts 'would have to learn much that has not been taught in England during the past three centuries' (quoted in Brinkworth 1943:95). The difficulties are immeasurably greater now. This book is meant to be a contribution to help those who wish to explore again worlds which we may not quite have lost, but are rapidly losing. It is to help the rapidly growing band of amateurs and professionals, from schoolchildren to the retired or redundant, who wish to uncover the workings of a past civilization.

Materials for the study of the English past
While a great deal of the material heritage in the form of buildings and fields has been destroyed and is being destroyed, much still remains. The same is true of the documentary records which are the subject of this introduction. The surviving English records are among the most continuous and diverse in the world. England is a small country, yet a number of factors made it create and keep more records than many large empires. The English have for centuries depended heavily on writing, on making records on paper and parchment. The reasons for this emphasis on writing rather than on oral tradition, as in so many societies, are too complex to analyse here, though historians and anthropologists have speculated on them (Goody 1968, 1977; Clanchy 1979). The unusual and early established central political and legal system, whose central courts and departments regulated life through written processes from the twelfth to nineteenth centuries, produced a vast body of material. Likewise, the presence of a landholding system that remained intact from the twelfth to nineteenth centuries produced, and retained for its later use, a mass of documentary material. These political and social forces which created the documents also led to the belief that old documents were still relevant to present

2

needs, hence preserving them in an unusual way.

The possibility of keeping ancient archives was increased by other factors. England has never been fought over by large destructive armies in such a way as to destroy large numbers of records nor have there been violent revolutions among whose aims was the destruction of all records of the past. Furthermore, the climate and the absence of record-destroying termites make record preservation moderately easy. It is possible to pick up a parchment or even paper sheet written five hundred years ago which is in better condition than paper in books printed during the last ten years.

Partly as a result of this superb survival of documents, but also one of the reasons why records survived, was the very ancient and active tradition of antiquarian research in England. The emphasis on precedent, on the relevance of the past in law and custom, combined with curiosity and a love of one's particular corner of England, led to an intense and early interest in research into early documents and physical remains of the past. The very survival and study of local records tells us a great deal about the attitudes of people in the past to time, to history, to writing and to one's locality. Thus one could partly explain both the survival and the study of documents by a cultural tradition which for over five centuries believed in the power of precedent, in re-affirming the customs of one's ancestors, a belief that an understanding of the past would guide the present. One could also partly explain the tradition in social terms; the presence of a large, literate, middling group of professional people, clergy, lawyers, minor gentry and others, both in London and spread throughout the counties, has led to the formation of numerous local history societies and has provided an active hobby for many. The energies which in some European countries have gone into the study of the 'folk', of their material culture and lore, now enshrined in the splendid folk museums of France, Germany and elsewhere, in England went into the study of documents, in the massive collections of

3

records in public, local and private collections.

Clearly the reasons for the compilation and preservation of past documents are much more complex than this. What is important for those setting out to re-discover the past is the fact that English records are continuous from a very early date, often from the thirteenth to sixteenth centuries onwards, that they are usually well organized and accessible, and that there has been a great deal done over the last hundred years to put them into print and to provide guides to their study. In the rest of this chapter we will outline briefly what has already been undertaken in some fields of documentary analysis and some of the aids already available for those setting out to re-discover the past.

The English tradition of antiquarian and topographical research
In practice it is difficult to distinguish between general antiquarian interest in past documents and research on the records of a particular place or topography. The greatest figures in each tradition have been identical, from Aubrey, Spelman and Dugdale through to Maitland and W.G. Hoskins. We will thus treat the two streams in English history together. Hoskins and others trace the interest in topography and local history back to William of Worcester, who made his tours of England to note down local antiquities principally in the years 1477-80 (Hoskins 1963:15). If we accept this starting point, then, as Hoskins argues, the study of English local history and topography is five hundred years old. Since that date, and probably before, the English have been keenly interested in their past and in their locality. In the sixteenth and seventeenth centuries there emerged that great tradition of topography and antiquarian research, a roll-call of whose names can be expanded in the work of Hoskins (1959:ch. 2), and on the antiquarian side in that of Pocock and Hay (Pocock 1957; Hay 1977:chs. 7,8). The great county historians included Saxton, Lambarde, Carew, Burton, Dugdale, Spelman, Dodsworth and Thoroton. The town historians included Stow, Butcher and Grey. The parish

4

historians included White, Kennett, Gough and Lucas. The
antiquaries included Camden, Aubrey, Dugdale and Spelman.

The early development of research into old documents and
physical remains can be judged in various ways. As early as 1572
the Society of Antiquaries was founded. By 1696 there was so much
work in this field that Bishop Nicolson could publish his English
Historical Library. Giving a Short View and Character of most of
our Historians either in Print or Manuscript: With an Account of
our Records, Law-Books, Coins, and Other Matters Serviceable to the
Undertakers of a General History of England (1696-9; 2nd edn 1714).
By the middle of the eighteenth century a very great amount of work
had been done and it was again surveyed, this time in Richard
Gough's British Topography: Or an Historical Account of What has
been Done for Illustrating the Topographical Antiquities of Great
Britain and Ireland (1768; best edition 1780 in two large quarto
volumes). The subject became so popular that a journal was started,
the Topographer, 'Containing a Variety of Original Articles,
Illustrative of the Local History and Antiquities of England...'
(1789-91).

Work in the field of local history and topography, delving
into and transcribing large quantities of records, continued apace
through the nineteenth century. The nature and quantity of work
published is indicated in four bibliographies. In 1815 Sir Richard
Colt Hoare published a catalogue of his magnificent library of
topography at Stourhead (Colt Hoare 1815), and three years later
William Upcott published a similar work on English Topography,
which provides a detailed collation of the works to that date
(Upcott 1818). In 1881 John Anderson published a classified
catalogue of all the topographical works in the British Museum (now
British Library) (Anderson 1881). Finally, there was Charles
Gross's Bibliography of British Municipal History (1897). Many of
the works noted in these bibliographies were based on detailed
archival research on private and public manuscripts. They often
contained lengthy transcripts of original records. Much of this

5

disparate work was regularized and systematized when the <u>Victoria History of the Counties of England</u> (still in progress with many volumes for some counties) began to appear from 1899, based on very extensive indexing of local and public records.

    The tradition which began in the fifteenth century has continued up to the present, and this century has produced some fine histories of counties, towns and parishes. The authors have often used sources which were unavailable to earlier antiquaries. This has been possible because of improved indexing and arranging of the records and the growing number of aids for those wishing to work on records.

The indexing, cataloguing and publication of English records
Many of the great antiquarians and topographers were themselves collectors of manuscripts or in charge of manuscript collections. In order to use their own and the public material it was necessary to order, index, catalogue and, preferably, publish the records. There were thus from very early on a number of serious attempts to survey and catalogue the records. In the years 1800-19 Commissioners appointed by the Crown surveyed the public records and in 1819 their two large volumes of <u>Reports</u> with appendices were published. This work was later taken up again and amplified in the numerous reports of the Historical Manuscripts Commission from 1874 onwards (see Stephens 1973:6, and Mullins 1958). These covered many private and local, as well as public, records, the public records also being described in the numerous <u>Reports of the Deputy Keeper of the Public Record Office</u> from 1840 onwards and in the lists, indexes, catalogues and guides (1963) published by the Public Record Office. The massive collections of manuscripts in the British Museum, Harleian, Sloane, Stowe and Additional, were calendared from the start of the nineteenth century onwards. The National Register of Archives issued reports and a visit to it is a useful part of any detailed study of a particular place or family. Indexes to certain types of documents, particularly probate

6

materials, have been published in quantity by the British Record
Society. Since the last war local record offices have been
re-organized and most of them now have published guides to their
records, an early example being Emmison (1969). The great English
libraries also have catalogues of their manuscript collections, for
example those at the Bodleian, Oxford, the University Library,
Cambridge, and the John Rylands Library, Manchester.

Many of the early antiquaries published substantial extracts
from documents within their works. Reports of law cases from the
late sixteenth century onwards were another source of original
documents in easily accessible form. The publication of original
documents was always one of the major concerns and thus publication
has been continuous since the sixteenth century. But the pace of
publication of original records increased very rapidly in the
second half of the nineteenth century. The texts published by the
official public bodies, the Record Commissioners and Public Record
Office, were then supplemented by the great national and local
record-publishing bodies. Exact transcripts of particular classes
of record such as court rolls or wills were made, often with a
scholarly introduction explaining how they came to be written.
Especially remarkable for their early date and quality are the
publications of the Camden Society from 1838 onwards and the Selden
Society from 1888 onwards, the latter under the inspiration of one
of the major figures in the drive towards the use and publication
of original materials, F.W. Maitland. Simultaneously with these
national societies, there was a growth of publications by local
societies. Among the earliest were those of the Chetham Society,
concerned with Lancaster and Cheshire, from 1844 onwards and the
Surtees Society, from 1835, for Yorkshire and Durham. Their
publications were joined for many other counties from the 1850s
onwards. A list of their works arranged by record society up to
1857 has been published (Mullins 1958), and for those who need a
list published under each type of archive, for example publication
of manor court rolls, there is an earlier list up to 1851

7

(Somerville 1951).

Many other record societies exist to publish other kinds of historical record. For instance in the period 1834-44 there were founded the Camden, Parker, Percy, Shakespeare, Aelfric, Caxton and Sydenham Societies, devoted to the editing and publication of historical and literary manuscripts (Dorson 1968A:44). Thus a very large amount of historical material is in print. There have also been other kinds of publication. All the surviving Elizabethan records for the whole of a large circuit produced by the clerks of Assize are being published under the editorship of J.S. Cockburn (Cockburn 1975B). F.G. Emmison has published substantial extracts from most of the Elizabethan records for the county of Essex (Emmison 1970-8). We have published on microfiche all the surviving located records for one English parish from 1400-1750 (Macfarlane et al. 1980-1). National historians have also published selected extracts from documents as teaching and research aids. The most famous and earliest of these was William Stubbs's Select Charters (1870), which went into many editions. This covered the period up to Edward I. For a later period G.W. Prothero edited statutes and constitutional documents for the reigns of Elizabeth I and James I (1894). This was later superseded by J.R. Tanner (1940) for the period 1485-1603, which has again been superseded by Elton (1960). Alongside these mainly political and constitutional selections there emerged a generation later similar extracts illustrating economic history. Bland, Brown and Tawney (1919) published a set of documents arranged under such headings as 'the manor', 'towns and gilds', 'rural conditions'. This was supplemented by further documents partly edited by Tawney and Power (1924). These have been updated recently by Thirsk and Cooper (1972). These introductions to records dealt with one delimited branch of history over a limited period. An attempt to cover most kinds of historical interest over the whole of English history in any depth necessarily leads to a massive publication. Such a co-operative work was edited by David C. Douglas in twelve volumes covering the period 500-1914.

The volume for 1485-1558, edited by C.H. Williams (1967), for example, is over one thousand pages long, but it contains useful bibliographies, as well as lengthy extracts from many sources.

Guides to the nature, use and reading of English documents
Nicolson's work of 1696 may be seen as the first attempt to provide a guide to those interested in using documents. This began a tradition which found expression in a number of nineteenth- and early twentieth-century guides which are still useful today. There is Richard Sims's <u>Manual for the Genealogist, Topographer, Antiquary and Legal Professor</u> (1856) and Walter Rye's <u>Records and Record Searching</u> (1888). Later a broad survey of the sources for national and local history was provided in Hubert Hall's <u>Repertory</u> (1920). There was also a simple guide for beginners in E.E. Thoyt's <u>How to Decipher and Study Old Documents</u> (1893). This early work has been developed in a number of guides, among the earlier and most successful of which is W.E. Tate's <u>The Parish Chest</u> (1946). There are useful guides by Redstone and Steer (1953), Pugh (1954), Celoria (1958), Hoskins (1959, 1967), West (1962), Emmison (1966) and Rogers (1977). The most comprehensive of the surveys of local records is by W.B. Stephens (1973). The longest and widest overview of English records is provided in two books by J.J. Bagley (1971) covering many sources with extracts from records, over the period 1066-1914.

These guides to documents are arranged either by type of document produced (parish records, probate records, lay subsidies, etc.) or by a general field of interest ('towns', 'education', 'agriculture'). Only one general author has recently written a survey, primarily of national records, which has divided the topic into the different institutions and hence the procedures which created the documents (Elton 1960, 1969). There have also been guides to particular document-producing institutions such as the Established Church (Owen 1970). There have also been a series of studies of particular records. An early move in this direction was

a series called 'The Antiquary's Books', which included works on
The Manor and Manorial Records (1906) by N.J. Hone and The Parish
Registers of England (1910) by J. Charles Cox. More recently the
publications of the Standing Conference for Local History, for
instance the guides to ordnance survey maps and folklore and local
history (Harley 1964; Phythian-Adams 1975), have been useful.
Likewise the Historical Association have published a number of
small pamphlets on particular records and topics, including two
indispensible publications entitled County Records (Emmison and
Gray 1961) and English Local History Handlist (Kuhlicke and
Emmison 1965). Further useful articles on sources and methods of
analyses are to be found in the journals The Amateur Historian
(later Local Historian), Archives (Journal of the British Records
Association) and the Journal of the Society of Archivists. The
journal History also contains from 1962 some helpful 'Short Guides
to Records'.

There are also a number of books which are more concerned
with the methodology of analysing particular documentary sources.
An introduction to the analysis of parish registers and listings of
inhabitants and the method of 'family reconstitution' is provided
by Wrigley and his associates (Wrigley 1966). A very useful
glossary to the demographic terms and techniques is Bradley (1971)
and to demographic sources and their accuracy Hollingsworth (1969).
We have attempted to provide elsewhere a general description of how
to reconstruct the history of a parish through the indexing and
combining of various records (Macfarlane, Harrison and Jardine
1977). Probably the most interesting way in which to discover how
to use such records and their potentials is through their use in
works by local and other historians. Among the more stimulating
recent studies are those of Britton (1977), Clark (1977), Hoskins
(1957A, 1963), Phythian-Adams (1979), Ravensdale (1974), Razi
(1980), Spufford (1974) and Wrightson and Levine (1979).

A number of the general guides to records include
transcripts of documents (e.g. Stephens 1973), sometimes with

photographs of the originals against which the transcripts can be compared, for example Emmison (1966), West (1962). These introduce the student to the records themselves and give some first hints on the problems of reading the old handwriting. But the deciphering of the old hand and translating the Latin is such a large problem that alongside the general guides there has grown up a class of aids to reading and deciphering the documents. One of the earliest of these, and much used in the nineteenth century, was Andrew Wright's Court Hand Restored, or, the Student's Assistant in Reading Old Deeds, Charters etc., first published in 1776. It has now been superseded by a number of guides which provide parallel photographs and documents and examples of script. Among the most useful are Hector (1958), Grieve (1954) and examples of documents published by the Borthwick Institute (St Anthony's Hall, York). The problems connected with the use of Latin abbreviations, grammar and vocabulary have now been dealt with in depth by a number of authors. Thus the works of Martin (1910), Gooder (1961) and Latham (1965) are standard tools for the person working on pre-eighteenth-century documents. Other useful technical guides include those to chronology (Powicke 1939) and to dating (Cheney 1970). The latter includes lists of major officials, the regnal years, the dates of movable feasts.

The need for a further introduction
The present introduction is thus one stone in an ancient and still continuing wall. It has been felt useful to provide it because the locating of material about the past, about a specific place, person, problem or period is both so fascinating but also such a lengthy and often expensive business that a short, cheap, introduction which explains the overall nature of English documents can be of use. Despite improvements in storage and indexing, records are still widely scattered over England and until the searcher has an idea of the way in which the records were created it is impossible to know where to look or to know what one will find. Furthermore,

even when material relevant to one's interests is found, it will be impossible to understand the meaning of the words on the page unless one has some idea of the procedures and of the writers who created the document. It is the aim of this work to provide a preliminary simple outline of the institutions in the English past which created the records that have survived, how they were interconnected, their scribes and process. If we are to proceed, we need to know for what purpose and with what assumptions the documents were written. Furthermore, we need to have some idea not only of what survives but of what else was written down at the time and has since been lost. At a deeper level, we need some understanding not only of what was recorded, but also of what was omitted because it was common knowledge or thought irrelevant. Clearly this can only be a preliminary introduction to the massive and complex archives now available. The interested reader will need to follow up the specialized literature which bears on the particular sources that interest him or her and which have been outlined in this chapter.

2. Some problems and limitations

The problem of preserving the continuity of English documents
In order to make any topic manageable it is necessary to draw
boundaries. Many historians draw narrow temporal boundaries,
perhaps studying a generation, a decade or even a single year. To
have limited ourselves in this introduction to even a relatively
long period, say the years 1500-1700, would have run against one of
the central features of English documentary evidence and of the
institutions which produced them, that is their immensely long
duration and continuity. When we examine the records of England as
a whole it is difficult to find any convincing period at which to
break off the survey. A realization of this continuity was one of
the reasons which led G.R. Elton to take the whole period 1200-1640
as a period of record-keeping (Elton 1969). Yet 1640 is not a major
permanent break and most series of records except those of certain
prerogative courts continue again after the Restoration up to the
nineteenth century. This is a problem which faced F.W. Maitland.
When considering the forms of action at common law Maitland devoted
one lecture to the period 1307-1833, that is between the accession
of Edward I and the changes in the parliamentary system (1832), the
legal system (1833) and the Poor Law (1834), which all occurred in
the 1830s and could be seen as a plausible stopping point. Maitland
ended his two-volume History of English Law at 1307 having shown
that many of the major principles and procedures, the
administrative and legal structure had already been laid down by

that date. He thus saw the next five hundred years as one integral period. He admitted that 'A period lasting from 1307 to 1833 is enormously long', but continued that 'I do not know that for our present purpose it could be well broken up into sub-periods' (Pollock and Maitland 1968:43). The same is true of any study of English documents. Indeed, as will be apparent throughout the central chapters of this work, many of the records we are concerned with started before 1307 and continued to be kept until the early part of the twentieth century. For example, the memoranda rolls of the Exchequer have survived for the period 1156-1926, approaching eight hundred years. Many of the central court series last for over six hundred years. We are thus dealing with a set of records with a continuous existence over a very long period.

This is not to argue that there was no change or even that change was unimportant. Obviously certain types of document only become general in the later centuries and others die out. There is clearly, as Elton has pointed out, a burst of new recording from the sixteenth century. But the impression of an archival revolution at that time is certainly partly caused by the better survival of records, combined with a growing population and greater wealth. Thus the quantity of records increased very considerably, but the nature and form of records does not change so dramatically. Since there is an inherent tendency to assume that there has been a dramatic change just before and just after the period under observation, we need a wide time frame to observe the evolution and development of English historical documents. We have therefore taken a very long period of over six hundred years, from the start of Elton's period of 1200 up to the end of Maitland's in 1833. As we shall see, the widening of this time frame has its cost, forcing us to narrow down in other ways.

The problem of preserving the interconnectedness of English records
A second striking feature of English institutions is their

interconnectedness. This partly arises from a very marked and
unusual degree of centralization of institutions. England is a
relatively small country which was early unified. The Normans and
Angevins re-inforced that uniformity and centralization which the
later Anglo-Saxon Kings had achieved; they bound every individual
and every institution to the Crown. The Crown, the Church and the
lords were blended in a complex overlapping system. In order to
understand the records and hence the history of England it is
necessary to consider the records as a whole. For the study of any
particular problem, place or person, it is essential to bring
together records created by several individuals or bodies. We need
to understand the way in which all these institutions fitted
together. For example, the care of the poor was for many centuries
the joint responsibility of the Church and the State in almost
equal proportions and their officers worked together. The
maintenance of law and order was the joint responsibility of those
who worked within the manorial and the Crown institutions. The
raising of revenue or the counting of the population was often in
the hands of all three authorities. Any individual was likely to be
involved in activities stemming from the demands of all three.

Given this situation, if we isolate a particular type of
record, for example a will, without considering how wills were used
within the manorial courts to devize property, we break the web of
understanding. Only by studying all the major institutions over
this long period will we gain a sense of the way in which layer
upon layer of records was created. These records dealt with
different aspects of the same person or event, for instance the
ecclesiastical authorities punished the bastard bearer for his
moral offence, the civil authorities for his economic offence if he
was unable to maintain the child. Through the overlap of such
records we are able to reconstruct the lives of thousands of
ordinary people in the past.

Indeed so interconnected were the institutions that any
attempt to split the records up into categories is artificial and

leads to a certain distortion. In reality the Church and State were indistinguishable in some areas, as, in the same way, the Church administrators were indistinguishable from the lords of the estates. Yet while this is the actual situation, it is clearly impossible to provide an introduction that does not treat one subject after another and hence classify. In order to reduce the interconnectedness of the reality of the past to that order required for a preliminary understanding, we are forced to set up divisions. Only after the artificial divisions have been mastered will a searcher be able to re-construct the wholeness. This necessity to create somewhat unreal divisions has been accepted by all those who have written descriptions of documents. Indeed most of them, by dividing their topics into much smaller units, for example specific types of archive such as court rolls, wills, parish registers, have preserved much less of the interconnectedness. One of those who has attempted to show how the various records of a particular institution fit together is G.R. Elton (1969). We have therefore adopted a modified version of the classification used by Elton. The major modification is that we have brought together the manorial records of the court leet and court baron as 'Estate' documents since they are inseparable in the rolls upon which they were recorded. Elton's classification, which treats them separately, is technically correct since the leet is a different jurisdiction. Other minor record-creating officials and institutions are fitted into a scheme which, like all classifications, contains certain anomalies and inconsistencies.

The choice of a particular case study
Given the need to study the records of England over a period of six hundred years and the desire to preserve their interconnectedness, it is clearly necessary to bound the study in some other way. The documents produced by a country with an average population of about five million inhabitants for this period are very extensive. It is clearly beyond the scope of a short introduction to describe them

all. It would require several lifetimes to become an expert on such
a broad range of material and many books to describe it. The
restriction we have decided to adopt is a geographical one. This
study is based on the description of the records for one English
parish, covering their interconnections over the period from the
start of such records up to the early nineteenth century. The
parish of Earls Colne in Essex was chosen because it was located in
a county whose records have survived particularly well and which is
favoured with an outstandingly well-organized record office; the
surviving records for that parish are unusually diverse and
voluminous. The records are not just described at the parish level,
for the search for references to one parish leads one to search
larger units, an archdeaconry, county or even group of counties. As
we shall see, there is a considerable problem in generalizing from
one instance and anyone interested in another county or parish or
problem will have to modify the description given here. Despite
this drawback, it was felt to be more helpful to give a description
based on a particular specific example rather than a vague brief
survey of all possible cases. We thus follow the method which has
been used by Hoskins (1957A, 1963) and West (1962) in earlier
introductions to the nature of documents. Since the choice of the
place will determine the range of documents which have been
described, and their survival, it is necessary to provide a brief
sketch of the nature of the parish whose records form the core of
this description.

The parish of Earls Colne
Earls Colne is named after the river Colne upon which it lies and
the Earls of Oxford who owned the manor from before the start of
our documents and who were often buried there. It is five miles
from the market town of Coggeshall, ten miles from Colchester and
about forty miles north east of the city of London. With a total
circumference of approximately ten miles and an area of just under
3,000 acres, it constituted a tiny part of the land area of England.

Some problems and limitations

Likewise its total population, which fluctuated between 500 and
1,200 persons during this period, only constituted roughly one
hundredth of the population of the county of Essex and one
ten-thousandth of the total population of England and Wales.

Earls Colne lies in the boulder clay plateau of northern
central Essex at a height of between 100 feet and 400 feet above
sea level, in an area of small hills and valleys. Although there
were traces of open-field cultivation in the fifteenth century,
most of the parish, like much of central Essex, had been early
enclosed into small fields with hedges. Most of the old forest had
receded, except for one large medieval woodland called Chalkney
Wood comprising about a fifteenth of the parish. There were also a
few alder groves and marshes, but most of the rest of the land was
used for mixed farming. The use of the land changed very greatly
during the period up to 1833. In the seventeenth century, for
example, the crops included grain, hops, fruit, and vegetables and
there were various kinds of animal husbandry. Although the river
Colne which formed the northern border was not navigable at this
point, its waters drove two mills. The main communications were
along roads to Coggeshall, Colchester and Halstead, including the
main Cambridge to Colchester road which ran through the village.
Much of the produce from the village was taken in this way down to
Colchester where it was carried by water to other ports, including
London. Apart from agriculture, the main occupations were
shop-keeping and petty manufactures. There was a fair on Lady Day
(25 March) and numerous shops and inns. There was a market place
with open stalls in the middle of the village. Occupations altered
very considerably through the centuries. As well as smiths, tanners,
millers and other occupations there were, particularly from the
later sixteenth century with the influx of Dutch immigrants into
north-eastern Essex, considerable numbers employed in spinning and
weaving cloth for export all over Europe. In all these respects,
Earls Colne was similar though not identical to other villages in
northern and central Essex.

The parish of Earls Colne

The size of the village fluctuated very considerably over
these three hundred and fifty years, from a lower limit of a little
over a hundred dwellings to an upper limit of twice that number. In
the map of 1598, there were 140 houses. Many of these were
subdivided. Two-thirds of the houses lay in the main village along
the street, the other third was scattered as farms and cottages
through the rest of the parish: a nucleated settlement pattern
characteristic of this part of Essex. There were also several
larger buildings: the parish church of St Andrew; the buildings of
the small Benedictine Priory of Colne which flourished until 1534;
the central residence of the lords of the manor which was several
times rebuilt, being moved from near to the church to the site of
the dissolved Priory.

When we turn to the landholding pattern, we find that less
than two hundred acres of Earls Colne was held by 'free deed' or
freehold directly of the King. The rest was held in two lordships:
the manor of Earls Colne and Colne Priory. During the period from
1137 up to 1583 the former was held by the Earls of Oxford as part
of the Earldom. The seventeenth Earl sold it in that year to Roger
Harlakenden, whose descendants have held it ever since. The other
manor, Colne Priory, was held by the Priory until 1534 and then
granted a few years later to the Earls of Oxford until they sold it
to the same Harlakenden family in 1592. Approximately two-fifths of
each of the two manors were let out to tenants by copyhold tenure,
the other three-fifths were held directly by the lords as demesne.
During the course of time, some of this land was formed into
largish farms usually of between fifty and one hundred acres such
as Hay House and Curds.

It is clear from the many surviving records that there was
very considerable social mobility in the parish, both vertical and
geographical. Many people spent only a few weeks or years there and
the boundaries of the parish were not strong barriers. Many owned
property both within and outside the parish. Kinship, commercial
and other ties cut across the parish boundary. We have thus chosen

19

a somewhat artificial entity, long recognized as the basic unit of
ecclesiastical and civil jurisdiction and, by chance, coinciding
more or less with manorial boundaries, yet not constituting a
closed and discrete 'community'. It is a geographical and
administrative space through which we can watch a tiny part of the
population of England move over the centuries. This particular
space was not chosen because it seemed in any way exceptional in
its social or economic situation, but because certain types of
record in which we are interested survived unusually well.

Most of the records for this parish are ones which must once
have existed for almost all the villages in England. But they have
survived particularly well through the antiquarian interests of
the Harlakenden descendants. The Carwardine and Probert families in
the nineteenth and twentieth centuries helped to save the very rich
manorial records from destruction. Earlier the documents had
survived through the energy of Roger Harlakenden, the first
purchaser of the lordships from the Earls of Oxford, who, involved
in lawsuits with the former owners, had many of the
fifteenth-century rolls and other documents transcribed -
manuscripts which have since disappeared. Another unusual source is
also a by-product of Harlakenden's activities, for in 1598 he
commissioned a detailed survey or 'terrier' of the whole parish
which was to be accompanied by a map. Both have survived and enable
us to place almost every field, house and barn in that year. Only a
few dozen such maps and surveys exist for anywhere in England
before 1600. His son Richard Harlakenden kept detailed accounts
relating to the estate, which were continued by his son Richard.
Such manorial estate books are also rare. Even rarer are diaries
kept by village inhabitants. Between 1641 and 1683 the vicar of
Earls Colne, Ralph Josselin, kept a diary which comprises 645 pages
in print, thus filling in many of those details which are missing
from other local records (Macfarlane 1976). Thus while it is
probably fair to say that if the records had been created or
survived we might expect to find a broadly similar range of records

for many English villages over this period, in practice in only a very few are we able to make such a study.

Problems of typicality and generalization

For those who have studied continental Europe, the idea of choosing one parish in one region and using this as a model for introducing the records of the whole country would seem absurd. The regional variations in culture, geography and society extend to the archives and consequently for the student of Languedoc in the sixteenth century, for instance, there is little to be gained, except by stark contrast, by a description of the records of Brittany. There is indeed a cost in the method we have followed in that each parish, archdeaconry, county and region was different. Yet there is little doubt that in terms of the nature of the record-producing institutions and the form of the records they produced, the variations over this whole period were surprisingly small. One consequence of that early uniformity and centralization, the presence of a common law, a common language and common political institutions, is that the records are also common or uniform. This means that despite regional differences in geography, ecology, agriculture and many other features, the documents produced over England are remarkably uniform, at least in outward form. Thus, to a certain extent, to describe the specific character of the records for one county and even for one parish, as we shall be doing, goes a certain way towards describing the general character of the records for all the counties and parishes of England. This is why as a student of Essex it is possible to draw great benefit from, as well as to feel no sense of strangeness at, the particular studies of records in Leicestershire (Hoskins 1957A), Worcestershire (West 1962) or Cambridgeshire (Spufford 1974).

Naturally there are variations in the precise processes and organization of the institutions in different areas. Thus those who read this introduction and work in a different part of England cannot simply apply the descriptions unchanged to other situations.

For example, we shall describe the ecclesiastical jurisdiction in
Essex and particularly in the Archdeaconry of Colchester. Those
working in a different archdeaconry and even more so in another
bishopric will need to adapt the description. For example, the
jurisdiction and processes in the Archdiocese of York were
different from that in Canterbury. Likewise the manor court
operated slightly differently in an early enclosed mixed arable
area like Essex from the way in which it operated in a highland
pastoral region or an open-field area of central England. Certainly
the officials and some of the terms and minor parts of the process
would vary.

Yet what is most striking in comparative perspective is the
very great uniformity and identity of documents over England. One
way to test this for oneself would be to read through the published
records edited for local record societies. Reading published wills,
inventories, parish registers, quarter sessions records, manor
court rolls, and other documents for selected areas in totally
different parts of England will quickly show to the student the
degree to which the records of one area are different from those of
another.

Our own experience is that there is a striking overlap in
terms, processes and organization of documents in contrasting
regions. To take just one example, we might cite the contrasts
between the work on Essex which is central to this description and
the work we have been doing in a region which is in every respect
as different from Essex as it is possible to find in England. This
is the parish of Kirkby Lonsdale in Westmorland. This is in an
upland, pastoral area of sheep-farming, where people lived in small
hamlets rather than in the nucleated settlements of lowland Essex.
It was at the opposite extreme of England from the influence of
London and its social structure appears to have been much more
egalitarian. We have transcribed the wills, inventories,
archdeaconry records, rentals, court rolls, parish registers,
archdeaconry accounts and other surviving documents for Kirkby

Lonsdale. They are almost identical in construction to the same classes of documents for Essex and there is scarcely a type of document which we know was made for one area that did not exist for the other. Obviously the details concerning individuals and their activities, the contents of the documents, varied very considerably. But the framework of documentation, which is our concern in this introduction, was broadly similar. Thus, for example, the judicial institutions and the records they produced are almost identical, while the types of offences for which people were accused were often very different (see Macfarlane and Harrison 1981).

This is not to argue that the surviving records will be the same all over England. There are very considerable differences between county and county and parish and parish because of the differential survival of records. This is much more important than the differences in the nature of records first created. For example, the records for Earls Colne and Kirkby Lonsdale look rather different at first sight because while many of them, for example wills and rentals and central court cases, overlap, each place has sources not found for the other. For Kirkby Lonsdale there are seventeenth-century listings of inhabitants, inventories of possessions and seventeenth-century church warden's accounts. None of these can be found for Earls Colne. In reverse, there are fifteenth-century account rolls and sixteenth-century manor court rolls for Earls Colne and none for Kirkby Lonsdale. Yet in each case this is due to the chance survival of records for we know that all these types of record were made for each area. This differential survival does mean, however, that the student needs to look carefully at the records of the county, bishopric and parish before he selects a specific area for work.

Documentary sources created by private individuals
One bias created by taking as one's central example the records about a particular place is that it draws us towards public records

and away from private individuals. That is to say towards material created by officers of institutions - parish clerks, ecclesiastical officials, clerks of Assize - rather than the private writings of past generations. In terms of quantity this bias is justified; such public records are immensely larger in quantity than private documents. Also, in terms of providing a general introduction to documents it is clearly easier to deal with formal public documents which follow a common form and whose interpretation depends less on the idiosyncrasies of a particular personality. Finally, while one needs to know a great deal about the personality, social and political position, and other specific characteristics of a letter writer or diarist, once one knows this it is relatively easy to read and understand in a preliminary way his or her writings. On the other hand, one cannot even begin to understand a lengthy deed, a manor court transfer or a set of presentments in an ecclesiastical court until one has a preliminary understanding of the institutional processes which created the document. For all these reasons the bias appears justifiable. But while private documents lack quantity and often appear relatively simple, they are nevertheless extremely important. Many of our most vivid insights into the past are not through the relatively formal public records, but in the private notes of travellers, diarists or letter writers. A very brief survey of these private documents is therefore necessary.

Although relative to public records private documents are less numerous, nevertheless papers written by individuals in their private capacity have survived in ever increasing quantities from the fifteenth century onwards. The most intimate of such documents are the daily or weekly journals and diaries. We have discussed elsewhere some of the reasons for the growth of diary-keeping from the sixteenth century onwards, varying from the religious desire to examine one's conduct to the aim of helping one's memory (Macfarlane 1970:ch. 1). There are a number of books written about English diaries in general (Notestein 1938, 1956; Ponsonby 1923,

1927), and an annotated list of diaries has been compiled by
William Matthews (1950). This lists, with place of publication when
they have been published, the famous diaries of Pepys, Heywood,
Evelyn, Woodforde and others and the numerous unpublished
manuscripts in public repositories. Many other manuscript diaries
undoubtedly exist in private hands or in manuscript collections
not surveyed by Matthews. Complementing these diaries and journals
are autobiographical accounts written in retrospect rather than at
the time, many inspired by religious sentiments. Some of these for
the seventeenth century are described by Delaney (1969) and a list
of published and unpublished texts has also been compiled by
Matthews (1955). In the sample parish on which this introduction
focuses we have a very good example of this general class of
material in the lengthy diary of the vicar of Earls Colne, Ralph
Josselin (Macfarlane 1976).

One occasion when people were especially likely to keep an
account of what they observed and what they thought was when they
travelled. Limiting ourselves merely to those who travelled within
Britain, there is a large amount of material which includes the
famous early published travels of such figures as Leland, Camden,
Fiennes, Defoe, Young and Cobbett. There are also many unpublished
travels. There are now extensive surveys and bibliographies of such
travellers, both of the English travelling round Britain (Anderson
1881; Burke 1942; Cox 1949; Moir 1964) and also of foreigners who
came to England and described what often struck them as its
peculiar people and institutions (Rye 1865; Ballam and Lewis 1950;
Wilson 1955). The shock of contrast between country and country or
region and region is especially valuable for historians. Another
class of literature of similar importance, but not considered here,
is the vast amount of documentation on the reactions of the English
to foreign travel and exploration, both at the amateur level of
interested travellers and as professional administrators and
anthropologists. Just as Samuel Johnson's travels to the Highlands
and Outer Islands of Scotland tell us almost as much about England

as they do about the place visited, so the reaction of colonialists and explorers, many of them unpublished, are invaluable for our understanding of the assumptions of the people who went abroad. Two pleasant introductions to this type of literature are provided by the Massinghams (1962) and Carrington (1947).

Diaries, autobiographies and travels all fall within the general class of autobiographical material. A second general class was what might be called family papers. Almost all public repositories of documents have deposits of private papers, usually from more prosperous gentry families. These often include letters, private household accounts, memoranda of various kinds, as well as copies of public documents. In Earls Colne, for instance, the papers deposited by the family of Harlakenden, who were lords of the manor for many generations, contain all these types of documents: marriage contracts, letters, account books, private genealogical notes. It is always worth searching through indexes of documents for such private papers. In our northern parish of Kirkby Lonsdale, the family papers of Sir Daniel Fleming and his descendants contain letters and account books, as well as copies of public business documents such as listings of inhabitants and the informal activities of a Justice of the Peace which are indispensable for the historian. Private letters alone constitute a large and important source of unpublished documents. Elton (1969:153-62) has provided an introductory description of some of the more famous collections of letters, a few of which have been published in their entirety. The Paston, Cely, Plumpton, Verney correspondence are only the outstanding early examples. Many other letters are catalogued or summarized in the numerous manuscript catalogues of the British Museum and in the Reports of the Historical Manuscripts Commission and National Register of Archives.

Alongside the letters are private accounting papers. These sometimes consist of single sheets of bills, receipts, of income and expenditure, or of paper books in the form of ledgers. They can in theory be treated as separate from the accounts of businesses, of estates, of merchant houses, gilds and boroughs. In practice, of course, there is often a good deal of overlap between private and public accounts. A particularly striking published example of an early private account book is that of Sarah Fell of Swarthmoor Hall (Penney 1920). Such accounting documents are jumbled together with other private materials and many of them lie in sacks of papers deposited during actions in the central courts, now in the Public Record Office. The vast wealth of material in such sources can be illustrated by the recent publication of the six-volume edition of the confiscated Lisle Letters (St Clare Byrne 1981).

Records produced by other institutions and corporations

By focusing on a parish and hence on the major national institutions through which it can be observed, namely the State, the system of Estates and the Church, another bias is created. The very extensive archives created by other lesser yet nevertheless important public bodies and corporate institutions are not treated in this introduction. This is another cost of our approach and the nature of what is being omitted needs to be listed.

One major category of records not specifically considered are borough, town or municipal records. Elton, who provides a brief introduction to such records up to 1640 (1969:119-28), divides such records into charters, court records, minute and letter books and accounts. He also stresses the diversity within these classes and the variations between boroughs. Clearly those who are interested in the history of English local government or who wish to study an area which either is a borough or includes such a borough will need to use such records and to work out the machinery of local government. Hoskins has discussed some of the sources and methods in this area (Hoskins 1959: chs. 6, 7), and a more detailed account of borough and gild records, with an outline of some of the printed and unpublished sources, is given by Stephens (1973:47-54). A recent example of what use may be made of good borough records is provided by Phythian-Adams (1979).

27

Records produced by other institutions and corporations

A second category is what Elton terms 'business archives', that is the records of companies and gilds (Elton 1969:16-24). Here we move from the records of the great trading companies such as the Levant and East India Companies, down to the records of small family firms and gilds. A detailed survey of the documentary sources in this field has been provided by Stephens (1973:ch. 5), where various classes of documents from trade directories to customs accounts, as well as the records specifically produced by gilds and companies, are analysed.

A third category consists of the documentary records of those bodies which might roughly be termed charitable, spiritual or educational institutions. Isolated examples of the records produced by some of these institutions will be mentioned in the survey of the three main institutions. In Earls Colne there was a Priory and some of the Priory records as well as some of those of the grammar school have survived. Yet this gives no true idea of the very extensive documents which have been created, and often particularly carefully guarded, belonging to religious or educational foundations. The archives of monastic orders, of schools, colleges, Inns of Court and universities are largely omitted in this introduction. The educational records are dealt with at length by Stephens, as are the records of Protestant and Catholic nonconformist groups (Stephens 1973:ch. 8).

Documentary sources outside the span of this introduction
We have tried to survey a very long period. Even so, there are major sources which have been omitted because they were written just before or after the ends of the survey. Before 1200 there are the chronicles, charters and, above all, Domesday Book. Each of these poses specialist problems which are beyond the scope of this work, as are the difficulties associated with manuscript literary sources before the fifteenth century. After 1833 one of the major sources for many historians are the manuscript enumerator's returns to the decennial national censuses from 1841 onwards.

Types of historical material not considered in this introduction

Furthermore, there are growing numbers of plans, maps and awards, created by enclosure, tithe and, later, Ordnance Survey officials. Such records are invaluable in piecing together the earliest history of England and they are especially important as the old boundaries and physical geography are altered out of recognition. Both Hoskins and Stephens in their guides provide an introduction to these important sources all of which have been indispensable in our own work on English parishes.

Types of historical material not considered in this introduction
If we wish to re-discover a rapidly vanishing society there are many types of material available to us. This introduction is exclusively concerned with only one category of material, manuscript or documentary sources. It is an introduction to information which still exists primarily in the form of written, rather than non-written, sources, and specifically with handwritten rather than printed or published sources. What has been excluded is just as important for a realistic understanding of the past as what is included here. It is therefore necessary to catalogue very briefly what is omitted entirely.

Printed and published primary materials of all kinds are not included here. This means that from the ephemera of almanacks, chapbooks, broadsheets and ballads, through sermons, pamphlets up to literature (poems, plays, novels), philosophy and science are not considered. Before 1640 there is a brief overview of 'Books and Writings' (Elton 1969: ch. 7), and after that period there is a vast secondary literature describing published sources. As printing was extended, and particularly from the eighteenth century onwards, printed sources become more and more important for even the most local of historians. Local newspapers, local directories and, above all, the very extensive published 'blue books' or parliamentary papers are of central concern. A brief introduction to these omitted records is provided by Stephens (1973:7-8,13).

This introduction does not deal with non-written sources for

Some problems and limitations

the understanding of the past. What anthropologists often call
'material culture', from the high arts of painting and music,
through to the construction of houses and fields to tools and other
artefacts, needs to be considered in a full appreciation of the
past. A local historian will use all the available sources. He will
consult the relevant volume of the Royal Commission on Historical
Monuments, examine the old buildings and engage in that local
fieldwork which has so well been described by Hoskins (1957B,
1959:chs. 8,18, 1967). Only by combining the written words of local
documents and the physical remains can a rounded picture be gained.

From the second half of the nineteenth century, which is
beyond the limits of this introduction, two new tools become
available to the historian. One is the record provided by the
camera. Old photographs and later old movie film become important;
a preliminary description of the former is again provided by
Hoskins (1959:ch. 3). The second tool is oral history. Our neighbour
remembers vividly being told about farming practices in the fens by
her grandfather, who was born in 1840. Thus the conversations and
reminiscences of townsmen and countrymen can carry us back at least
140 years. Such oral history has been used to great effect by
social historians, for instance in the works of George Ewart Evans
(1960, 1970, 1975, 1976). The potentials and difficulties in using
oral history and oral tradition in a literate culture are discussed
by Vansina (1973), Thompson (1978), and in the journal Oral History
(1970 on). One class of material which cross-cuts the divisions we
have made, but is often associated with oral history, is what Thoms
in the nineteenth century christened 'Folklore', that is to say the
proverbs, sayings, old rites and ceremonies of a passing
civilization. Phythian-Adams (1975) has argued for the value of
such material for local historians, and a broad survey of British
folklore studies and their sources has been provided by Dorson, who
has also provided a two-volume selection from the great
folklorists (1968A, 1968B).

This then is a very preliminary introduction to some of the

Types of historical material not considered in this introduction

documents of some of the major institutions in the English past.
Rather than providing a survey of all materials, or even of all
manuscript sources, this work takes a long time period and
investigates the central connections of the major three
institutions. This may seem unduly constricted, but within its
particular aims, and given the difficulty of its central subject
matter, it is hoped that it will prove useful. It is believed that
once the core institutions of State, estates and Church are
partially understood, it will be easier to fit in those smaller
institutional records, those private accounts and those published
and non-written sources which are indispensable for the endless
task of recreating the past.

3. Records of the State

The central legislative and judicial institutions are the King in Parliament and the King in Council. The King's will is transferred in action principally through the Great Seal held by the Chancellor, hence the records of Chancery. His government is financed through various offices, principally those of the Exchequer. His peace is maintained through the common law courts, King's Bench and Common Pleas foremost amongst them. The defects in justice are remedied through the equity courts arising out of his Council, particularly Chancery. His peace is further maintained through the Commissions of the Peace issued to Justices. These branches of government are highly integrated, of great antiquity and sophistication. They were largely established by the end of the thirteenth century. Though they were developed, elaborated and modified, they remained recognizably the same until the nineteenth century. The law here administered was the common law of England, including statute, plus the system known as equity. This law was enforced by officers from the village constable at the lowest level, up through the High Constable, the Justice of the Peace and Sheriff, up to the most powerful men in the land, the Chief Justice of England, the Chancellor and the King. The records which this system created survive from the twelfth to the nineteenth centuries and are the most majestic and continuous set of governmental archives in the western world. They provide an immense amount of material concerning the integration of every parish in

Government and administration

England into a highly centralized and bureaucratic nation state
from an early period. Yet the records are so vast and complex that
only a tiny fraction of them have as yet been used by either local
or national historians. In the following description it will only
be possible to show very generally what exists between 1307 and
1833. All the records described in the sections before 'Commissions
of the Peace' are deposited in the Public Record Office, Chancery
Lane, London. The Record Office class numbers are given in brackets.

Government and administration

Parliament and Council
The most important decision-making institutions in the realm
were the King in Parliament and the King in Council. This produced
the massive archives of Parliament, particularly the Journals of
the Commons and Lords. Parliamentary proceedings and statutes
affected every parish very considerably, but it is unlikely that
very much specifically concerning one parish will be found in the
surviving records before the middle of the eighteenth century.
Equally important was the King's Council, which advised the King,
helped in the ordinary administration and acted as a court of
appeal. Many of the Council records have been lost or were
destroyed by a fire in 1619. From 1540 onwards there exists a
continuous series of 'acts' or minutes of the Privy Council; the
published calendars reach the year 1631.

Chancery
The central institution which carried out the will of the
King in Parliament and in Council was the Chancery, the Chancellor
being in charge of the Great Seal of England which authenticated
orders and decrees. The importance, as well as some of the
functions, of Chancery was well summarized by Chamberlayne.
> This court is the officina justitiae, the womb of all our
> fundamental laws, the fountain of all our proceedings in law;
> the original of all other courts. It is as ancient as the

33

> civility of the nation...Out of this court are issued writs,
> or summons, for Parliaments and Convocations, edicts,
> proclamations, charters, protections, safe-conducts...patents
> for sheriffs, writs of <u>certiorari</u>, to remove records and
> false judgements in inferior courts...Here are sealed and
> enrolled letters patent, treaties and leagues with foreign
> princes, deeds between party and party, touching their lands
> and estates, or purchasers taking recognizances, and making
> of extents upon statutes and recognizances for payments of
> money, or securing of contracts, writs remedial or
> magisterial, commissions of appeal, oyer and terminer etc.
> (Chamberlayne: 111).

The records produced by this branch of government were kept 'very
professionally, with much system and care' (Elton 1969:35) from the
end of the twelfth century onwards. Only a general idea of what
might be contained in them can be given here. There are some 200
rolls of 'charters' (C.53) from 1199 to 1516, which contain copies
of the formal grants by the Crown, for example the right to hold
markets, the incorporation of towns, the right to hold certain
courts. There are some 5,432 'patent' rolls (C.66) from the period
between 1201 and 1944. They contain a very wide and diverse set of
public grants made in open (patent) letters to individuals and
corporations, including 'presentations to churches and chapels,
creations of nobility, special and general pardons, special
liveries, licences and pardons of alienation...' (Guide:22). These
contain the enrolments of letters close, called this because they
were issued folded and 'closed' by the Great Seal. There was also a
growing tendency to use the back of these for the enrolment of
private deeds. There are the massive number of 20,899 'close' rolls
(C.54) between 1204 and 1903, though from about 1540 the rolls are
blank except on the back. There are some 553 'fine' rolls (C.60) from
1199 to 1648. These were rolls upon which 'were entered the
payments, in money or in kind, offered to the King by way of
oblation or fine for the passing or renewal of charters or grants,
and for the enjoyment of lands, offices, wardships, exemptions,
liberties, privileges, and other marks of the royal favour...'

(Guide:19). The other main class consists of the warrants which the Chancery received. Many of these have been lost, but many also survive. For example, from the period from Henry VII to Anne, there are some 360 bundles (C.82). There are also numerous classes which could contain material. For example, there are 146 bundles of 'miscellanea' (C.47) of the Chancery, which contain many types of record: special commissions, ecclesiastical documents, writs and returns from Chancery. Almost all of these documents were written in Latin, on rolls which each contain many hundreds of feet of parchment.

One class of documents produced by Chancery requires separate attention. These are what are known as <u>inquisitions post mortem</u>. The Crown could, through the use of the Great Seal, order a great many enquiries to be carried out, known as inquisitions. One of the chief reasons for such inquisitions was to examine the situation after the death of people who held land directly of the King, typically by knight service where the tenant was 'in chief'. If such a tenant died without an heir, his land escheated to the lord. If there was an heir he could not take legal possession of the land until he had paid a relief, roughly equivalent to a year's rent. During any minority, the King took the revenues of the estate and could dispose of the heir or heiress in marriage. In order to exploit these important sources of revenue, special officials were appointed from the middle of the thirteenth century onwards to investigate the circumstances at the death of each tenant in chief. A writ was sent to these men, directing them to take possession of the lands of the deceased, to summon juries of local free men. These inquisitions gave rough ages, which have been used by demographic historians. Acompanying the inquisitions there are also extents or valuations. These, because of the uncertainty of their accuracy, have usually been omitted from the published calendars of inquisitions, though they are often very valuable for historians. The inquisitions continued to be taken until the end of feudal tenures in 1660. The originals were sent into Chancery; some 1,847

files survive for the whole period (C.132-C.142). Copies, which are
often in better condition, also exist for many of these in the
Exchequer (E.149,E.150) and in the Court of Wards and Liveries (WARD
7), another 1,577 bundles in all.

Secretary of State
One other governmental archive, which complements that of
Chancery, was that created by Secretaries of State, a heterogeneous
collection called 'State Papers'. These cover a wide range of
topics, but they are unsystematic in content and survival.
Furthermore, they only preserve incoming correspondence. Elton has
given a good account of their virtues and defects (Elton
1969:66-75). The originals are in the Public Record Office (S.P.)
and there is a published calendar.

Finance

The Exchequer
There were several financial organs of the government, but
pride of place must be given to the Exchequer. Its records are vast.
As Elton points out 'the Guide to the Public Records devotes
sixty-nine pages to what is little more than a list' of these
records.

> The mass is so enormous that research on it will never end;
> the information is so multivarious that nothing, one feels,
> that happened in the realm could possibly have escaped
> record; the technical difficulties are such that very few
> scholars have ever mastered more than a part of these
> sources; and compared with the Chancery, very little has so
> far been done to make the records accessible in print (Elton
> 1969:46).

All that we can do here is broadly to sketch a few organizational
features of the system and the records which they produced. Broadly
speaking, the Exchequer was divided into two parts. The Lower
Exchequer (or Exchequer of Receipt) was concerned with the actual
receipt, collection, storing and issuing of the revenue. The Upper

Exchequer (or Exchequer of Account) audited the accounts of the receivers of revenue.

Exchequer of receipt

The Lower Exchequer's records are vast. For example, there are 2,620 rolls and volumes of 'enrolments and registers of receipts' (E.401) between 1160 and 1866, and 3,109 rolls and volumes of 'enrolments and registers of issues' from the reign of Henry III (mid-thirteenth century) to 1834 (E.403), as well as many other volumes and books. There is a huge array of records, with no obvious calendars and indexes to help entry into them. Only a very detailed knowledge of Exchequer procedure would make it possible to interpret what is found, for there are considerable complications in the system of duplicate book-keeping employed (Elton 1969:48).

Exchequer of account

Somewhat more accessible, but even more daunting, are the records of the Upper Exchequer. During the centuries there were considerable changes in the composition of and divisions within the Upper Exchequer, but for the present purposes we can distinguish between three main branches, the Pipe Office, the Lord Treasurer's Remembrancer, and the King's Remembrancer.

Pipe Office

The Pipe Office kept the oldest and grandest master record of all, the great roll of the Exchequer or Pipe Roll, which was continuous from 1155 to 1833. Later it became so bulky that it was split into separate series so that the so-called 'foreign accounts' (those rendered by anybody except the Sheriffs) were split into customs accounts, accounts of subsidies, declared accounts and so on. Thus there are 676 Pipe Rolls (E.372) from 1131 to 1832, 3,617 rolls of 'declared accounts' from 1500 to 1810 (E.351), as well as many other, smaller, collections. As the business of the Pipe Office grew more complex, it spawned other offices. The two main ones arose out of the existence of debts (outstanding items), of which the

Exchequer needed to be 'reminded'. Hence the creation of two further
record-keeping departments: the Lord Treasurer's and the King's
'Remembrancer'. Elton writes that 'since their main purpose was to
remind the Exchequer of outstanding business, their contents are
miscellaneous and illumine all sorts of matters connected with the
revenues' (Elton 1969:49). Their purpose was to proceed against
defaulting persons, to institute enquiries, and to verify claims
for allowances, etc.

Lord Treasurer's Remembrancer
We may deal first with the Lord Treasurer's Remembrancer,
which developed in the late twelfth century and which, as an office,
had its duties first defined in Ordinances in 1323. This office was
more particularly concerned with fixed revenues, mainly from land,
of the types that had existed in the twelfth century. The major
class of record produced are the memoranda rolls (E.368), some 804
rolls from 1218 to 1833. There are also some 131 volumes of
'miscellaneous' books' (E.369), 154 bundles of 'miscellaneous rolls'
(E.370) and 1,102 originalia rolls (E.371) made in Chancery for the
information of the Exchequer. The memoranda rolls, for example:

> include proceedings relating to the accounts of sheriffs,
> escheators and bailiffs, from the fines, issues and
> amercements contained in the rolls of estreats returned into
> the Exchequer from other courts, from writs...and from the
> seizure of lands belonging to recusants. These rolls also
> contain the enrolments of deeds...From the sixteenth century
> the sheriffs' cravings for allowance of expenses provided
> some information about the holding of Assizes and Quarter
> Sessions, including the custody of persons awaiting trial and
> the execution of convicted felons (Guide:75).

As with most of the major Exchequer records, they are written in
abbreviated Latin on huge parchment sheets.

King's Remembrancer
By the same Exchequer Ordinances of 1323, the duties of the
King's Remembrancer were officially defined. Among these was:

> to enrol all deeds, charters, and recognizances of debts made
> or acknowledged before the Barons and to issue any
> consequent writs of execution. He was to keep extents
> returned into the Exchequer, particulars of accounts
> rendered...rolls of taxation granted by the clergy or the
> laity, rolls of attermined debt (for the recovery of which he
> was to issue writs)...He thus became primarily responsible
> for the collection of the casual revenue of the Crown...
> (Guide:49).

The Lord Treasurer's Remembrancer, on the other hand, had dealt with
fixed revenues from lands, etc. The ensuing records are vast. At the
heart of them are the memoranda-rolls, 789 of them between 1156 and
1926 (E.159). Among their contents are the following:

> transcripts of outlawries and other proceedings whereby
> lands or goods were forfeited to the Crown; special
> commissions of inquiry with the returns thereto;
> informations of intrusion on the royal forests and wastes;
> and enrolments of enclosure awards. From the 16th century
> onwards they also record informations of offences against
> the various statutes regulating trade and industry and of
> goods seized for non-payment of customs (and later also of
> excise) or for unlawful importation... (Guide:62).

Like the Lord Treasurer's Remembrancer rolls, the documents are
physically very large. They consist of strips of parchment,each
over two feet long, with writing on both sides, and about five
hundred strips per roll. They are mainly in Latin, though there are
by this time some English depositions.

There are numerous classes of subsidiary documents. As Elton
(1969:47-8) wrote: 'masses of accounting documents, subsidiary to
the final statements, survive in a class called, despairingly,
"Accounts, Various" (E.101). It took a folio volume of 351 pages to
list the main bulk of them. There are numberless files of writs for
payments, and archives of papers produced by investigations.' For
example, just one category of records are 'fines and amercements'
from Henry III to Anne which are described as 'chiefly accounts of
fines and amercements before Justices of Assize, King's Bench,
Common Pleas and Forest, Barons of the Exchequer, and Justices of

the Peace in various counties...' (Guide:51).

The most accessible and obviously useful category of
material is the set of documents relating to taxation. The main
series are the subsidy rolls (E.179), with which we will be
concerned shortly. As a background to these, there were numerous
series, of which we may mention a few. There are some 462 bundles of
'certificates of residence' (E.115) from Edward VI to Charles II
which certified that the persons named were, at the time of a
particular assessment, resident at the place specified in the
certification, and had there been taxed. They were originally
attached to returns now in the Lay Subsidies. There are nearly 1,500
bundles of 'receivers accounts of land and assessed taxes' (E.181-3)
between 1689 and 1830. These include parchment duplicates of totals
paid by parishes in the land tax, as well as many other
certificates and miscellaneous papers.

The 'lay subsidy' rolls (E.179) are the most widely used and
accessible of the Exchequer records. During the period between 1400
and 1750 the two types of tax which generated the largest number of
names for a locality were the lay subsidies and the hearth tax. The
lay (that is, non-clerical) subsidies were first introduced in
1523. In the collection of the first two years (1523, 1524) they
covered a large proportion of the adult male population, but
thereafter they fell on a diminishing proportion of the population.
There is considerable discussion as to what can be deduced from the
various categories in these subsidies; for example, Stephens has
argued that the 'number of persons paying tax only on wages will
indicate the size of a landless labouring class. But it must be
noted that the adolescent sons of yeomen and husbandmen were
assessed on "wages" though not really of the labouring class'
(Stephens 1973:110). The documents themselves are arranged by
parishes on narrow membranes, and written in lists, in Latin.

As the needs of the Crown continued to grow and its revenue
failed to keep pace with inflation, other expedients were tried.
One of these was 'ship money', in which an attempt was made to tax

the whole country, including the new commercial wealth. The 1636 assessment for Essex (S.P.16/358) contains many local names. The most useful of all the taxes for a local historian was the 'hearth' tax, which was levied from 1662 to 1689. The care with which taxation was undertaken and the need for careful inspection can be illustrated more generally by a description of the process in this particular tax.

By an Act of 13-14 Charles II c.10 (1662), every householder who owned property worth 20s a year or more, and was not otherwise exempted by poverty, that is by the receipt of alms or relief, was liable for 2s a year for every fireplace or stove in his house. Returns of lists of persons were ordered to be made to the Justices of the Peace by the constables and tithing-men. One copy was to be enrolled by the Clerk of the Peace and a duplicate sent to the Exchequer. Every owner or occupier of a property was ordered within six days of receiving notice from the constables to 'deliver unto the said constables...a true and just account in writing under the hands of such owners or occupiers'. If there was no such return, or the officials were not satisfied with the statement, the constables were empowered to search the house. If the person paid the tax, the constable was to give an acquittance; if he refused to pay, his goods were to be distrained. If the person was living in a house under the value of 20s. per annum and did not have property to that value, then the churchwardens and overseers of the poor were to write out a certificate to that effect. As with all other taxation documents, it is a difficult matter to deduce much from them. But, generally speaking, a small number of hearths can be used as an indicator of a small house, and exemption can be used as an index of a certain poverty. Where a return does not have the exemptions specified, it is not possible to use these returns in order to estimate total population.

The other major tax, which was later to become so important, only appeared towards the end of the period, namely the land tax. This was voted annually from 1692 onwards. The totals by parish

survive in the Exchequer (E.181-3), but it was not until 1780 that a
list of the names of those assessed had to be deposited with the
Clerks of the Peace and have hence survived in local repositories.
Before that date only a few of the Assessment Books which give the
names of the persons paying the tax, have been deposited in local
Record Offices.

There were a number of other offices which were either
closely or loosely attached to the Exchequer. One was the Treasury
of the Receipt of the Exchequer. This contained not only the chests
that held the King's money and jewels, but also the most valuable
parchment records, such as Domesday Book, Assize Rolls and various
court rolls. There are many deeds, miscellaneous books and other
materials here, as well as certificates of the military musters.

General Surveyors and Augmentations

Parallel to the system of finance through the Exchequer was a
system whereby the Crown dealt with its finances through the
Chamber. An ancient tradition was regularized by the Statute of 3
Henry VIII c.23 (1511), whereby 'General Surveyors and Approvers of
the King's Lands' were appointed. The effect was 'to remove the
receipt and audit of the greater part of the revenues of the Crown
from the purview of the Exchequer to the hands of the King's
personal servants' (Guide:80). The Court of Augmentations and Court
of General Surveyors were later merged. They created massive
records during their existence, particularly as a result of the
confiscation of monastic lands. There are, for example, 527 volumes
of 'miscellaneous' books (E.315) and many volumes of the proceedings
of the court (E.321). The Court of Augmentations was abolished in
1554 and its business was taken over by the Auditors of the Land
Revenue. It produced a large set of records. For example, there are
421 bundles and volumes of 'views of accounts' (L.R.8), as well as
court rolls and 371 enrolment books of grants, leases, warrants,
etc. (L.R.1).

First Fruits and Tenths, Wards and Liveries

Two other important prerogative or statutory courts were set
up by Henry VIII to deal with the revenue. One was the Court of
First Fruits and Tenths, which was to receive clerical payments.
This business was later put into the hands of the Exchequer. The
surviving records are, relatively, few in number, being
approximately the equivalent of 300 volumes and bundles in all
(E.331-E.344). The other prerogative court, set up formally by the
Statute of 32 Henry VIII c.46 (1540), was that of Wards and
Liveries. This dealt with the rights of the King over his tenants
in chief, that is their wardship during a minority and their
marriages. The records include 700 volumes of 'miscellaneous' books
(WARD 9), 174 bundles of pleadings (WARD 13), 55 boxes of 'deeds and
evidences' (WARD 2) and 53 bundles of 'feodaries surveys' (WARD 5).

Only a tiny fraction of the financial records of the State
have been indexed or calendared. What treasures await the historian
in the remaining material it is difficult to say, but it is
important to realize that the financial fragments which have been
recovered are only a small part of what survives, which in turn is
only a part of what was once written down.

Common law courts

The system of English government and finance rested, ultimately, on
the common law. Sir Matthew Hale stressed that the common law 'is
not only a very just and excellent law in itself, but it is
singularly accommodated to the frame of the English government, and
to the disposition of the English Nation, and by such as by a long
experience and use is as it were incorporated into their very
temperament and, in a manner, become the completion and
constitution of the English Commonwealth' (Hale 1971:30). He
continued as follows:

> This law is that which asserts, maintains, and with all
> imaginable care, provides for the safety of the King's Royal
> Person, his Crown and dignity, and all his just rights,
> revenues, powers, prerogatives and goverments, as the great

foundation (under God) of the peace, happiness, honour and
justices, of this kingdom; and this law is also, that which
declares and asserts the rights and liberties, and the
properties of the subject; and is the just, known, and common
rule of Justice and Right between man and man, within this
Kingdom (Hale 1971:30-1).

The matters which it dealt with are also well summarized by Hale.

This is that law by which proceedings and determinations in
the King's ordinary courts of justice are directed and
guided. This directs the course of descents of land, and the
kinds; the natures, and the extents and qualifications of
estates; therein also the manner. forms, ceremonies and
solemnities of transferring estates from one to another. The
rules of settling, acquiring, and transferring of properties;
the forms, solemnities and obligations of contracts; the
rules and directions for the exposition of wills, deeds and
Acts of Parliament. The process, proceedings, judgements and
executions of the King's ordinary courts of Justice; the
limits, bounds and extents of courts, and their
jurisdictions. The several kinds of temporal offences, and
punishments at common law; and the manner of the application
of the several kinds of punishments, and infinite more
particulars... (Hale 1971:17-18).

The law was called 'common' because it was general to the whole
kingdom; its roots were in the laws of the Angles, Saxons and Danes,
modified and strengthened by the Normans and Angevins. The praise
of Edward Coke was repeated by Jacob (1744:s.v.common) as follows:

The common law is grounded upon the general customs of the
realm; and includes in it the law of nature, the law of God,
and the principles and maxims of the law; it is founded upon
reason; and is said to be the perfection of reason, acquired
by long study, observation and experience, and refined by
learned men in all ages.

The common law was divided into two major branches, that
concerned with actions between the Crown and an individual, known
as 'pleas of the Crown', and actions between individuals, known as
'Common pleas': 'pleas of the Crown are all suits in the King's name,
for offences committed against his own crown and dignity, and also
against the peace, as treasons, felonies, mayhem etc. And Common

pleas are those that are agitated between common persons in civil cases...' (Jacob 1744:s.v.common). The process in these two types of plea was slightly different, though there was great similarity across the various courts whose jurisdictions we shall be examining. In pleas of the Crown, the procedure consisted in essence of the bringing of an indictment or formal charge written in Latin, presented on behalf of the King, to the Grand Jury. This jury would then either find it 'true', that is technically accurate, as a bill and the person to be suspected of the crime, or would dismiss the charge. The Crown would then have to prove the case before a petty or trial jury which would pronounce the person to be guilty or not guilty, and the judge would then sentence the offender. In civil cases, the procedure was more complex, reflecting the major stages in any case, namely the method of bringing the case to the court's attention, the enquiry into the case, the proof (or 'trial' as it was known) and the decision and enforcement of the decision. The common law action would begin with the plaintiff suing out a writ from Chancery (the 'original' writ), which enabled the relevant court to hear the case. Only if a person's troubles fell within these recognized 'forms of action' could he find a remedy. The 'mesne process' or machinery for bringing a person into court to answer the charge 'was exceedingly cumbersome and afforded vast opportunities for dilatory tactics' (Elton 1960:149). When the case came to be tried, it was pleaded in front of the judges in a form of law French, though these pleadings were gradually being supplemented by documents. The use of mainly oral trial methods meant that the whole case had to be reduced to a specific point of dispute (the issue). By the fifteenth century, the only method of trial or proof widely used was by the jury, originally of local freeholders. The judge would then give sentence. Thus the major differences from the Crown pleas were that the original writs were brought in by plaintiffs, rather than on behalf of the Crown by the Grand Jury.

This form of process and the way in which it was recorded

have made the central documents produced in these courts difficult
to use. From the middle of the fourteenth century, at the latest,
the plea rolls were fixed in a rigid form. As Elton puts it:

> They effectively record only the regular sequence of
> instruments under which actions were started (original
> writs) and the trial of cases was conducted (process out of
> court)...in Common Pleas and King's Bench the business was
> written up day by day, so that one has great difficulty in
> tracking the history of a given case through the rolls. All
> entries follow common form and tell almost nothing of the
> personal or individual facts behind a case: one will be told
> the names of the parties and usually their employment or
> status, and one is likely to discover the cause alleged in
> dispute, but that is all (Elton 1969:59).

They are consequently daunting records to use, but, as we shall see,
they can be supplemented by other classes.

The common law was enforced and administered by a number of
courts whose overlapping jurisdiction is confusing, and constantly
changing over time. To simplify very considerably, the most
important court for the hearing of pleas of the Crown was the
King's Bench. Judges also held assize commissions under which they
tried Common pleas in the locality (by process of nisi prius). They
came also to hold commissions of oyer and terminer and of gaol
delivery: these enabled them to hear pleas of the Crown (criminal
jurisdiction). The most important court for civil litigation was
known after the type of action as the court of Common Pleas (Common
Bench). Common law jurisdiction was also claimed by the two great
governmental departments, Chancery and Exchequer. At the lower
level, and to be dealt with elsewhere, were the local franchises,
the courts leet and courts baron, which, as we shall see, acted in
minor cases of the kind that came to the central or circulating
courts.

King's Bench

The most powerful of the common law courts, excepting
Parliament itself, was the court of King's Bench. 'For the execution

of laws, after the house of Lords in Parliament, the highest court
in England at common law, is the King's Bench, so called, because
anciently the sovereign sometimes sat there in person on a high
bench...' (Chamberlayne 1737:109). Chamberlayne continues that

> In this court are handled the pleas of the Crown, all things
> that concern the loss of life or member of any subject; for
> then the King is concerned, because the life and limbs of the
> subject belong only to the King. Here are handled all
> treasons, felonies, breach of peace, oppression,
> misgovernment etc. This court moreover hath power to examine
> and correct errors in <u>facto</u>, and in <u>jure</u>, of all the Judges
> and Justices of England in their judgements and proceedings;
> and this, not only in pleas of the Crown, but in all pleas,
> real, personal, and mixed, except only in the Exchequer
> (Chamberlayne 1737:110).

In recognition of this supremacy, the chief judge of the court was
popularly known as the Lord Chief Justice of England. It was thus
primarily concerned with actions between the Crown and individuals,
but from the reign of Elizabeth onwards the monopoly of the court
of Common Pleas in actions concerning property 'was threatened by
the various fictitious devices used by King's Bench to extend the
quasi-criminal action of trespass into a general civil
jurisdiction' (Elton 1960:148). Thus its records contain many
Common pleas between persons.

The surviving records of this court constitute a formidable
collection. They are divided roughly into the records of the Crown
pleas (Crown side) and Common pleas (Plea side). We will here
discuss only a few of the records of the Crown side. The major
series are the <u>coram rege</u> rolls (K.B.27), of which there are 2,149
extending from 1273 to 1701. These are a continuation of an even
earlier series, the <u>curia regis</u> rolls (K.B.26), some 234 rolls
between 1194 and 1273. The difficulties of using these plea rolls
have already been mentioned. They are written for the most part in
Latin, though some of the later depositions are in English. The
cases are split apart and continue over several rolls. There are
some indexes to the rolls, however, principally the 'controlment'

rolls (K.B.29), of which there are some 503 between 1329 and 1843.
These consisted of memoranda compiled for the use of the King's
Attorney and cross-refer to the coram rege rolls.

Another set of King's Bench records are those known as
'ancient indictments' (K.B.9-11). The King's Bench not only acted on
business brought directly to it, but also had the power to remove
indictments, presentments, and convictions from other courts,
particularly from those two jurisdictions, the Justices Itinerant
or Assizes, and the Commissions of the Peace, or Quarter Sessions,
to whom it had delegated power. By a writ of certiorari, that is a
'writ issuing out of the Chancery to an inferior court, to call up
the records of a cause there depending, that justice may be done
therein, upon complaint that the party who seeks the said writ hath
received hard usage, or is not like to have an indifferent trial in
the said court' (Jacob 1744:s.v. certiorari, quoting Fitzherbert),
King's Bench called in many of the records of the inferior courts.
These records survive from the end of the thirteenth century until
the middle of the nineteenth century. Also filed with these
documents were the returns of Coroners, that is their inquests on
all sudden deaths. 'By 1500 most coroners were surrendering copies,
in the form of individual indentures, of all their inquests, into
cases of homicide, suicide, death by misadventure and natural
death...for two and a half centuries after 1500 the records of
King's Bench contain copies of almost every case of every coroner'
(Hunnisett 1961:116).

Assizes
Very closely associated with the King's Bench, employing the
same judges and process and dealing with similar cases, were the
Assizes. The itinerant judges acted during our period under four
separate commissions issued out to them. The commission of assize,
after which they were named, enabled them to deal with ejectments.
An ejectment is an action that lies with a lessee for years who is
ejected before his term of years expires, and was developed in the

seventeenth century into the main way of trying titles to freehold
estates. The commission of <u>nisi prius</u> enabled the judges to deal
with civil cases similar to those which King's Bench managed to
attract through the fictions of trespass. The commission of oyer
and terminer enabled them to deal with treasons, felonies and
trespasses, and that of general gaol delivery with the prisoners in
gaol. The judges also sat as Justices of the Peace, by virtue of a
Commission of the Peace. This system of travelling Justices was
well established by the middle of the thirteenth century and it
continued until the middle of the twentieth. There were only slight
alterations to the circuits: for most of the period there were six
of these in England. Essex lay in the 'Home' circuit. There are many
records for this circuit in the archives of the medieval Justices
Itinerant. Fortunately, the later records of the Home Circuit are
the earliest surviving files from the sixteenth century for
England.

The major surviving documents from the sixteenth century are
the indictments, which commence in 1559 (ASSI 35). Such indictments,
like the indictments in other common law courts, have to be treated
with considerable caution since the details concerning time, place,
occupation and status are often somewhat misleading if taken at
their face value (Cockburn 1975A). Yet they are still useful since
they give us essential detail concerning offences such as murder,
robbery, burglary and grand larceny, and the other serious offences
with which the Crown or criminal side of the Assizes were
concerned. But we need to remember that what has survived in this
archive is only a tiny fragment of what once existed. Cockburn
estimates that the Assizes in session produced at least ten classes
of record: for Essex throughout this period, only one of these ten
classes, the indictments, have survived in any quantity (Cockburn
1975A:216).

Common Pleas
The major court for the trial of civil pleas was that of

Common Pleas, of great antiquity but only established formally by
Magna Carta to sit at Westminster. It had a universal jurisdiction
throughout England and was the primary court for the trial of
disputes between persons, particularly those cases concerned with
real estate. According to one authority, the court's jurisdiction

> was exclusive in the real actions, that is, those involving
> rights of ownership and possession in land; in the older
> personal action of debt, detinue, account and covenant; and
> finally, in mixed actions, both personal and real, such as
> ejectment. Jurisdiction was shared with the King's Bench in
> maintenance, conspiracy, other breaches of statute, trespass,
> trespass on the case, and their derivatives (Hastings
> 1971:16).

This was true of the fifteenth century, though it is clear from
statistics by the same author that at least in the reign of Edward
IV over three-quarters of the cases concerned the recovery of debts
(Hastings 1971:27). Another large category was that of trespass. The
court was active from the twelfth to the nineteenth centuries and
hence created a vast set of archives.

The records are indeed daunting. The central records are the
plea rolls themselves (C.P.40). There are some 4,135 rolls between
1273 and 1874, constituting approximately a million feet of
parchment, written mostly in abbreviated Latin and with the process
scattered across the rolls, often giving only a summary of the case.
A single roll could easily contain more than seven thousand
entries, many hundreds for a single county. Another important class
are known as 'final concords' or 'feet of fines' (C.P.25). But since
these are in fact documents produced when individuals used the
court merely as a registry for the transfer of freehold lands, it
is more appropriate to deal with them alongside deeds and other
estate records and their nature will be described there.

Exchequer of Pleas and Chancery (Latin side)

There were two other courts which dealt with civil suits or
common pleas at the national level. One was the branch of the

Exchequer known as the Exchequer of Pleas. Originally this had been
concerned with revenue cases, but in a similar development to that
of King's Bench it managed to use a legal fiction to bring in a
growing amount of business from the sixteenth century. Anyone
indebted to the Crown could 'sue upon a suggestion of quominus, that
is, of his being "the less" able to satisfy the Crown by reason of
the cause of action he had against the defendant...the application
of the writ of quominus was eventually so far extended that
practically anyone might institute in the Exchequer proceedings in
any personal action and in ejectment' (Guide: 92). This court also
had special powers in the Palatinates, Wales, Ireland, the Cinque
Ports and Channel Islands. Although the amount of business
transacted here was never as great as that in King's Bench or
Common Pleas, there is still a very considerable archive of
material, for example some 209 volumes of bills and writs (E.5) and
1,499 rolls (E.13) from 1236 to 1875. There are also a small number
of rolls and bundles recording the activities of Chancery as a
common law court.

Equity and conciliar courts
Equity is defined to be 'a correction, or qualification, of the law
generally made, in that part wherein it faileth, or is too severe.
And likewise signifies the extension of the words of the law to
cases unexpressed, yet having the same reason...' (Jacob
1744:s.v.equity). 'Equity' or 'fairness' was a principle and system of
justice which was gradually evolved to provide flexibility and
refinement to the framework of common law which has already been
described. By the later fifteenth century the common law courts had
several disadvantages. Chancery had not continued to create new
writs valid in the courts, so that a person could only find remedy
in the courts if his difficulty lay within the recognized and
circumscribed 'forms of action'. As Maitland put it, the common law
held that 'where there is no remedy there is no wrong' (quoted in
Elton 1960:149), thus reversing the normal principles of justice.

Furthermore, the procedure at common law was both long and
cumbersome; it encouraged obstructions, delays and large expenses.
These and other difficulties led to the emergence of a parallel set
of courts which grew out of the King's Council and were hence also
known as 'Conciliar' courts, operating a more equitable
jurisdiction. They developed originally under the eye of the
greatest legal official in the land, the Lord Chancellor, and hence
Chancery remained the main equity court, although the Exchequer
developed an equity jurisdiction during the sixteenth century.

   At the start, 'equity' was not a system, but 'simply the name
given to the sum of spasmodic decrees issued by the Chancellor in
individual cases of hardship, where either common law provided no
remedy, or the remedy had proved inadequate or abortive' (Hanbury
1944:128). But during this period the procedure became more
elaborate and in order to understand the important documents which
these courts produced, it is necessary to outline this process.
Firstly a bill of complaint was filed. This was a petition for
redress, written in English, in which all the grievances could be
elaborated. After the bill was filed, a subpoena was issued which
compelled the defendant to appear and answer the charge. This was a
vital weapon in the hands of the equity courts, for it avoided
those long delays found in civil cases in the common law courts.
The subpoena could be worded vaguely, ordering a person to appear
to answer 'whatsover may be objected'. The defendant then put in his
or her answer to the complainant, another written document in
English. Then the plaintiff could bring in his replication, unless
he filed exceptions against the answer as insufficient, referring
it to a Master to report. Exceptions could also be made against the
report. These replications and rejoinders were often merely
repetitions of the original bills and answers. If necessary, the
process could continue with a rebuttal and surrebuttal, but
normally the case would then move to the stage of issue or proof.
This consisted of the examination of witnesses who had to answer to
a set of written interrogatories, either in London or by commission

in the country. These witnesses were chosen by the two parties and
made written depositions, on oath. In complicated cases special
commissions could be granted and a group of officials would spend
days or weeks gathering evidence in the locality. A day would then
be set down for the hearing, after which followed the decree of the
Lord Chancellor. There was, it will be seen, no jury system and the
whole procedure relied heavily on written documents and was in
English. This makes the documents it produced many times more
usable and valuable for the historian than those created in the
normal course of events by the common law courts. The proceedings
could be terminated at any time if the parties could agree and it
is clear that one of the main aims of the procedure was to lead to a
reconciliation and a compromise.

The type of business which the equity courts dealt with was
very wide and varied. It can negatively be defined as concerning
all those matters about which people could dispute but which did
not fall within the province of ecclesiastical law, criminal law,
or the law of real estate. 'Real' actions, those in which the loss of
landed property might be the outcome, could only be heard in the
common law courts, and since the punishments which the equity
courts could inflict (fining and imprisonment in the Fleet), could
not be extended to the death penalty or the taking of possessions
(distress), they could not deal with felonies. But this left them a
vast area, principally centred round the question of trust and
covenant and breach of faith: the 'scope of equity jurisdiction was
well expressed under the three comprehensive headings of "fraud,
accident, and breach of confidence"' (Hanbury 1944:129). A general
description of the wide range of business which was dealt with by
Chancery by the end of the seventeenth century is given by Jacob.

> It gives relief for and against infants notwithstanding
> their minority: and for and against married women,
> notwithstanding their coverture: in some cases a woman may
> sue her husband for maintenance; she may sue him when he is
> beyond sea, &c...All frauds and deceipts, for which there is no
> redress at common law; all breaches of trust and confidences;

and accidents, as to relieve obligors, mortgagors, &c. against
penalties and forfeitures, where the intent was to pay the
debt, are here remedied...Also this court will give relief
against the extremity of unreasonable engagements, entered
into without consideration; oblige creditors that are
unreasonable, to compound with an unfortunate debtor: and
make executors, &c. give security and pay interest for money
that is to lie long in their hands...Here executors may sue
one another, or one executor alone be sued without the rest;
order may be made for the performance of a will: it may be
decreed who shall have the tuition of a child: this court may
confirm title to lands, though one hath lost his writings;
render conveyances defective through mistake, &c. good and
perfect... copyholders may be relieved against the ill usage
of their lords; inclosers of lands that are common be
decreed; and this court may decree money or lands given to
charitable uses...oblige men to account with each other
(Jacob 1744:s.v.chancery).

This is just a selection of the types of action that might come to
the court.

Court of Chancery

The largest and the most long-lived of the equity courts was
Chancery. The records of this court have never been explored in any
great depth and only part of them have been indexed. Following the
process of the court, we may divide these records into three stages.
The original bills, answers and further replications, etc., which
are often known as 'proceedings'; the examinations and depositions;
and the final decisions of the court. The 'proceedings' have been
most fully indexed and survive fairly well. These proceedings
(C.1-C.10) survive from the late fourteenth century, and there are
some 7,000 bundles up to the year 1714. There are another 3,000
bundles in the years 1714-58 (C.11). Each bundle contains up to 200
or more 'cases', each case consisting of one or more large parchment
sheets, some two foot by two foot or larger. There are thus probably
over two million 'cases' up to the middle of the eighteenth century.
There are reasonable indexes, either printed or in manuscript, to

about three-quarters of the documents up to 1714. A record of the
progress of the cases which were initiated by these bills and
answers is kept in process books termed 'decree and order' books
(C.33). There are many hundreds of these volumes from the sixteenth
century onwards. In certain cases the original proceedings were
referred to one of the Masters in Chancery for a report. A few of
these reports survive from the Elizabethan period, but they grow
numerous in the seventeenth century (C.38).

The next major stage in those cases which proceeded this far
was the interrogation of witnesses. Each party could set out a
number of questions to be put to one or more witnesses. If the
examinations were taken in London they were called 'town'
depositions (C.24), if outside London, then 'country' depositions
(C.21,C.22). There are some 2,509 bundles of the town depositions
from 1534 to 1853, perhaps a ratio of one to every four of the
proceedings. There are almost as many country depositions. In some
cases, copies of relevant documents were shown in court. Bundles
numbering 2,500 of those 'master's exhibits', which were never
reclaimed (C.103-C.114), survive from the thirteenth century.
Likewise, there are some 5,000 bundles of 'master's documents' from
the seventeenth to the nineteenth centuries, containing
'affidavits, examinations of witnesses, accounts and other
documents on which the Masters founded their reports, together with
the drafts of the reports' (Guide:31).

The final stage was the decision of the court and the decrees
it made. Whereas the proceedings and depositions have survived
relatively well, many of the decrees have been lost. Nevertheless, a
good deal remains. There are 2,500 decree rolls, containing decrees
and orders, stretching from the early sixteenth century to 1903
(C.78,C.79).

Court of the Exchequer
The equity jurisdiction of the Exchequer developed during
the early sixteenth century. Its procedure was similar to the other

equity courts and it obtained its business 'on the bare suggestion' that a person who filed a bill was the 'King's accountant' (Guide:48), for it had originally been a court especially for the King's servants. The records of this court 'have remained virtually intact' (Bryson 1975:86), being stored among the records of the King's Remembrancer. Like other equity records, they are in English, except for the formal patents, writs and endorsements. The major series reflect the original stage in the process, some 2,386 portfolios of bills and answers (E.112) from Elizabeth I to 1841. There are good contemporary indexes to these bills and answers. The cases were concerned with financial matters, particularly disputes over tithes.

As regards the next stages, the interrogatories and examinations of witnesses, there is also a good deal of material. There are 163 bundles of depositions taken before the Barons of the Exchequer (E.133), Elizabeth I to 1841, which are equivalent to the 'town' depositions of Chancery. There are 834 bundles of depositions taken by commission (E.134) which are equivalent to the 'country' depositions in the Chancery. There are also 246 bundles of 'exhibits' from the seventeenth to the nineteenth centuries (E.140). Finally there are 200 bundles of 'informations' (E.148) from Henry VII to 1923, which before 1842 were also enrolled on the memoranda rolls of the King's Remembrancer (E.159). These again largely concern drainage, enclosure, tithe and other agrarian matters. The final settlements by which these actions were ended were also recorded on the rolls. The other source for the final decisions are the more than 600 bundles of decrees and orders of the court, either the originals or entry books, from 1558 onwards (E.123-E.131).

Court of Star Chamber

One of two relatively short-lived courts arising out of the King's Council was Star Chamber, which grew in power and influence from the early part of the sixteenth century. By a process of

English bill addressed to the King, the court 'might make process
against maintainers, rioters, persons unlawfully assembling, and
for other misdemeanours, which through the power and countenance of
such as did commit them lifted up their heads above their faults,
and punish them as if the offenders had been convicted at law, by a
jury &c.' (Jacob 1744:s.v.Star Chamber). It will be seen that this
was a court particularly concerned with serious offences
concerning the peace, and particularly the matters of riots and
assemblies. It continued to function until it was dissolved in
1641. In many ways its records are easier to use than those of
Chancery and Exchequer equity courts, for the documents created by
various early stages in the process were not filed separately. Thus
a Star Chamber case sometimes consists of a huge bundle, often more
than fifty sheets in all, with the original bills, answers, replies,
subsequent interrogatories and examinations. But there are also
ways in which the records are less helpful. One is the result of a
loss of records: most of the documents for the first half of the
sixteenth century and the reign of Charles I have been lost. The
entry books which recorded the court's decisions have almost all
disappeared since the Civil War. The second disadvantage is the
absence of a reasonable calendar to the largest bulk of records.
Only fifty-seven bundles of proceedings have survived before the
reign of Elizabeth (STAC1-STAC4). By far the largest collection are
the 1,027 bundles of Elizabethan proceedings (STAC5-STAC7). There
is only an index of personal names, giving plaintiff and defendant.
The surviving Jacobean cases (STAC8) are only a quarter of the
quantity, some 312 bundles. But they have been fully calendared.

Court of Requests
The other relatively short-lived conciliar court was
Requests, which operated over almost exactly the same years as Star
Chamber, and used a similar process to the other equity courts. It
dealt with similar matters to Chancery, but was regarded as a poor
man's court. Its procedure was swifter and cheaper than that of the

other courts, and this attracted a growing flow of litigants. Much
of its business was concerned with such matters as enclosure, rack
renting, rights of common and the customs of the manor, though it
also dealt with many other matters. It exercised a 'civil
jurisdiction comparable to the criminal jurisdiction of the Star
Chamber' and it 'eventually took cognizance of almost every kind of
complaint...' (Guide:148). Like Star Chamber, its records were filed
in such a way that the original bills and answers and subsequent
interrogatories and examinations were kept together.

A great number of the original bills, answers and deposition
materials have been lost. There nevertheless survive some 829
bundles of proceedings between the late fifteenth century and 1640
(REQ 2). There are typed or manuscript indexes to the first 415 of
these bundles, giving place, name and subject. There are also 38
bundles of 'miscellaneous' proceedings (REQ3) and 210 volumes of
'miscellaneous' books (REQ1), that is affidavit books, appearance
books, note books, order books, process and witness books, none of
which have been calendared.

We have concentrated here on the manuscript records produced
by the courts themselves. Normally these are found in the Public
Record Office, but depositions, exemplifications and various
narratives prepared for cases in the high courts are also often
found in private deposits in local record offices. These records
can be supplemented and expanded by contemporary printed and
unprinted extracts and reports, which are particularly important
for the common law records. The most important of these are the
'Year' books. These are: 'In form a collection of notes on cases
which the note-taker had attended as an uninvolved onlooker, they
offer a great deal of information not only on the law but on many
aspects of life' (Elton 1969:174). Their content and difficulties
are well indicated by Elton (1969:174-80). There are very many of
them; for example, one survives for almost every year from 1307 to
1602. Especially for the later period, they are practically unused:
'no one has ever used the unprinted Year Books compiled after

1536...' (Elton 1969:176). From the early part of the sixteenth
century a new set of records, the 'Reports' began to be published.
These were less concerned to give the details of ordinary life and
speech that are embedded in the Year Books, and concentrate more on
points of law. Yet the famous reports, particularly those of
Plowden Dyer and Coke, do contain detailed accounts of the
arguments in cases which no longer survive in the records. More
informal than the reports are the contemporary accounts, growing
numerous from the middle of the sixteenth century, which were
written in the form of pamphlets for the literary market. They
principally dealt with bizarre or macabre cases. There were also
chapbooks and ballads. Many of them describe cases at criminal
courts or scenes at the execution which cannot be reconstructed
from other sources.

Commissions of the Peace and Quarter Sessions
Majestic and continuous though the central administrative,
financial and judicial institutions might be, they were matched by
the organization of administration, finance and justice at the
local level, without which they could not have worked. Much of the
burden here fell on the local gentry, given power through special
commissions, issued annually. The power, longevity and uniqueness
of this system is summarized by Maitland.

> Certainly to any one who has an eye for historical greatness
> it is a very marvellous institution, this Commission of the
> Peace, growing so steadily, elaborating itself into ever new
> forms, providing for ever new wants, expressing ever new
> ideas, and yet never losing its identity...we shall hardly
> find any other political entity which has had so eventful and
> yet so perfectly continuous a life. And then it is so purely
> English, perhaps the most distinctively English part of all
> our governmental organization (Maitland 1911:470).

General Commissions of the Peace for the whole country were
established by Statute in 1327, though before that time there were
specific commissions to particular gentry at certain times from at
least the later thirteenth century. The institution continued in

essence unchanged until the twentieth century. The Justices were
appointed shire by shire, year by year. The Tudors added greatly to
their administrative offices: 'during the sixteenth century this
old system of local law-enforcement was vastly expanded and
allowed to engross virtually all local government...' (Elton
1960:453). Their power derived from a number of Statutes as well as
from the commissions. 'By the end of Elizabeth's reign Lambarde
could list 309 statutes which in one way or another referred to the
duties of the justices of the peace' (Elton 1960:454). Some of their
powers by the eighteenth century are summarized by Chamberlayne.

> Their offices is to call before them, examine, and commit to
> prison, all thieves, murderers, wandering rogues, those that
> hold conspiracies, riots, and almost all other delinquents,
> that may occasion the breach of peace and quiet to the King's
> subjects...They are also impowered to put many Laws and
> Statutes in execution, and act in a judicial capacity, as in
> cases relating to the poor; the preservation of the same; the
> repairs of high-ways; the punishment of vagrants and other
> dissolute and disorderly persons (Chamberlayne 1737:125).

The Justices were thus involved not only in judicial matters, being
the rung below the national common law courts, but were also
responsible for such matters as the regulation of process and
wages, licensing, the maintenance of bridges and highways, the
enforcement of laws against religious nonconformity and the
supervision of the Poor Laws. Other business included the
supervision of the collection of taxes, the examination of weights
and measures, and many other duties which will become clearer when
we examine the specific records they created.

The Justices acted in two ways, either in general sessions,
or out of session, as individuals, or in combination.

> Every quarter, or three months, the justices meet...and there
> the Grand Inquest, or jury of the county, is summoned to
> appear, who upon oath are to enquire of all traitors,
> heretics, thieves, murderers, money-coiners, rioters etc.
> Those that appear to be guilty are by the said justices
> committed to prison, to be tried at the next Assizes, when the

judges go on their circuits... (Chamberlayne 1737:125).
Other non-judicial business was also transacted at what came to be
called the Quarter Sessions. But it was also possible and necessary
that a great deal of ordinary business should be transacted outside
and between sessions, either by Justices, or by the various
officials such as High Constables, Constables, churchwardens and
overseers of the poor, who were responsible to them in various ways.

Very considerable as the sessions records often are, they
comprise only a very small part of what was committed to paper from
the early fourteenth century onwards. As Elton writes 'the records
of the courts held by justices of the peace [quarter sessions]
begin patchily after 1540; though more carefully preserved from the
reign of Elizabeth onwards, they are never very complete in the era
here considered [i.e.to 1640]' (Elton 1969:56-7). If the records of
the courts are patchy, the surviving records concerning the equally
extensive activities of the Justices out of sessions and of their
unpaid local assistants are practically non-existent, what remains
being just a pitiful remnant of what once existed. We thus
constantly need to remind ourselves that what has survived,
particularly before 1560, only represents a tiny part of what was
once written down. In studying Essex, we are extremely fortunate,
for the Essex sessions records are among the earliest and the most
complete in the country. Diverse and voluminous documents,
surviving from 1556 onwards, are deposited in the Essex Record
Office at Chelmsford. We may divide them into the records of the
'court in session' and others.

Court in session
The most important documents concerning the activities of
the court in session are the sessions rolls (Q/SR), almost complete
from 1564 and consisting of approximately 100,000 rolls between
that date and 1850. The most common documents are presentments by
the two Justices of various offences such as failing to repair
roads, failing to attend church, keeping unlicensed or disorderly

alehouses and other 'nuisances'. There are also presentments by High
Constables and constables concerning servants, alehouses, archery
and other matters. These presentments concerned minor offences.
More serious offences or felonies were dealt with in an exactly
similar way to that in the other common law courts, by bringing
bills, which were confirmed or rejected by the Grand Jury. The most
commonly indicted offence was larceny. Accompanying the
indictments are informations or indictments by informers,
recognizances to secure the appearance of a person at the sessions
to answer a charge or give evidence, recognizances of licensed
alehousekeepers and others for good behaviour. There are also jury
lists and panels for the juries, calendars of prisoners in gaol,
lists of Justices present at the sessions, maintenance orders for
bastardy cases and individual petitions of inhabitants. These are
the most common types of document, though many others also exist.
Much of the most formal business was recorded in Latin, on
parchment. But many of the informations and presentments are in
English, often on paper. After a while the rolls became so bulky
that another parallel series, containing some indictments, but
mainly consisting of depositions and petitions, became established.
Between 1610 and 1750 there are over 15,000 documents in this
series (Q/SBa,Q/SBb). There are full calendars of the sessions
rolls, with place and person indexes, which makes them relatively
easy to search. But there are no such calendars of the bundles.

Alongside these major series there are smaller classes which
record aspects of the court business. The most important of these
are the sessions books (Q/SMg), which are minute books of the
sessions and which survive for scattered years between 1632 and
1750. There are also order books (Q/SO), which survive for 1652 to
1661, 1671 to 1686, 1698 to 1750, and contain the formal orders of
the court relating to both administrative and judicial matters.
Thus they deal with petty offences, bridges and highways, licensing
and the poor law. Other volumes contain extracts of fines,
summaries of indictments, lists of cases taken from the Quarter

Sessions to be tried at the Assize or King's Bench by a writ of certiorari. The survival of these sources is poor, and they mainly date from the later seventeenth century. Their contents are fully described in the Guide to the Essex Record Office (Chelmsford, 1968:9-11).

Justices out of session

The other main category of records are those concerning the various administrative and other duties of the Justices out of court. There are records of finance, for example accounts for the collection of rates and money for the repair of bridges (Q/FAac,Q/FR), and of the assessments for the hearth tax (Q/RTh). There are a number of enrolled private deeds (Q/RDb). There are recognizances for various kinds of tradesmen properly to carry out their trades, particularly victuallers (Q/Rlv). One important source is the 'association' rolls. By the Act of Association, 7-8 William III c.27 (1696), every office holder was to subscribe in court to the form of an oath 'for the better preservation of his Majesty's royal person and government' (Q/RRo2). All those who were likely to hold offices, including those of churchwarden and overseer of the poor, were also required to take the oath of loyalty.

Unfortunately, the numerous accounts and other documents which must have been kept by every Justice, High Constable and constable, have been almost entirely lost. The loss is well known at the level of the Justices, but is equally tragic at the level of the village constable. Their important role in tax collection has already been mentioned, but they were also vital in the keeping of the peace. They clearly had to keep accounts and write many kinds of order and certificate. Twice a year they had to answer a long list of enquiries concerning the state of their parish. Many other aspects of local government are reflected in the largely unsearched papers of local landowners. One other source under this general head of local government can also be mentioned. This is the printed poll books, which indicate the ways in which parliamentary electors cast their votes. Only freeholders were listed.

4. Records of estates

The documents produced by the owners of estates are the most
voluminous of English records. This is partly because property and
property law lay at the heart of English law and society. It is also
because the meaning of an 'estate' was much wider and more embracing
than it might be today. It encompassed not only rights in objects,
land and housing, but also rights in and over people, for instance
the rights to certain services and the rights to hold courts. Thus
a manor consisted not only of such things as 'house, arable land,
meadow, pasture, wood, rents, advowson ...' but also of 'services and
of a court baron' (Jacob 1744:s.v. manor). Thus when we survey the
records of an estate we are often dealing with matters with little
direct bearing on rights in land.

The rules which governed the holding and transmission of
estates, as well as the decisions in the courts held by individuals
who were lords of an estate, were based on a mixture of the common
law and local custom. The principles upon which law and custom
operated were very similar. The basic difference was that customs
were specific to certain places, while general customs constituted
the common law. A custom must be ancient, must have continued
without interruption, must be certain and must be reasonable. It
must also apply to a group of people, not just one individual, and
must not be against the King's prerogative. We shall see some of
these principles in action in the ensuing description.

We may very roughly divide the owners of estates into two

categories, those who held directly of the King, either as lords of manors or as holders of 'freeholds', and those who held of some intermediary lord. The latter consisted mainly of those who held of a lord of a manor, leasing a house or part of a demesne, or holding by copyhold or customary tenure. The registration, trying and transmission of these various titles absorbed a great deal of the time of the contemporary courts and created vast quantities of records. Lords of manors also created through their stewards and bailiffs a number of other major classes of records. They needed to know what their rights were, so they conducted frequent surveys of various kinds. They needed to know what their income, expenditure and profit was, so they kept elaborate accounts. Finally, the various courts which they kept required a record of their decisions. We may look at these categories of records in more detail, especially as they have survived for Earls Colne.

Surveys of rights
The foundation for all successful holding of estates was an accurate assessment of the resources and rights held. Detailed instructions on how to make such descriptions had been widely available from at least the late twelfth century. There were, in theory, five different and overlapping ways in which estates were surveyed. There were 'extents' or terriers, which listed holdings, duties of tenants and sometimes described the crops and livestock. There are numerous extents from the thirteenth to the seventeenth centuries. These became more elaborate, and topographical descriptions began to be given with the names of adjacent owners. They came to be called 'surveys' in the sixteenth century. The final method was to add a map. These are rare in the sixteenth century, and therefore we are exceedingly fortunate to have a fine map for Earls Colne made in 1598. But maps become more common in the seventeenth and eighteenth centuries.

These general descriptions were supplemented by two other devices. One was termed a 'rental'. This gave the tenant's name, his holding and the rents and services due from him. These rentals were probably made, or at least renewed, each year, in order to make it possible to ensure that the maximum profits were flowing in from the manor. They were made throughout England from at least the thirteenth century. The earliest surviving rental for Earls Colne manor was made in 1395, for Colne Priory in about 1400. Between then and 1750 another seventeen rentals, either for a single manor or for both, have survived. They are sometimes written in house order within the village and can hence be used in topographical reconstruction. A final description is the 'custumal', which sets out the customs of the manor, for example the rights of widows or daughters, and the rights of customary tenants on the common.

From these descriptions it is possible to build up a picture of the major estates at various points in time: 'they offer a clear understanding of how the land was laid out, how it was supposed to be used, and what it was supposed to yield to the lord, so that they can give an unusually systematic, if intermittent, picture of rural conditions, population, agricultural practices and the like' (Elton 1969:147). The documents are often very lengthy; it has been estimated, for example, that the rentals for the two manors in Earls Colne between 1380 and 1880 contain over 30,000 names. They must also be treated with caution, especially in the case of early extents. Nevertheless, they provide an indispensable framework within which other estate documents may be fitted.

Accounts

The only accounting documents which have survived in any quantity in connection with estates are those produced by lords of manors. These may be divided into two categories. There are the professional accounts kept by various officers employed by the lord, then there are the private estate accounts kept by the lord himself. The former, chiefly made by stewards and bailiffs, were by far the most voluminous. There are the account rolls themselves, made and audited each year, showing expenses, receipts and profits.

They were written in Latin on long parchment strips. Of the many
hundreds made for the manors in Earls Colne after 1400, only a few
such 'compoti' have survived, but they are of extraordinary
interest, showing in some cases even the daily diet of some of the
monks. They give receipts from rents and from fines in the courts,
sale of produce and sale of stock. They give the expenses of the
purchase of agricultural equipment, upkeep of buildings, wages for
agricultural work. The profits were then calculated and paid over
to the lord. Many subsidiary documents were used in drawing up
these accounts. Notes were made on the court rolls themselves,
giving the fines and amercements, the totals of expenses and income
from a particular court. The fines were also extracted from the
court rolls onto other rolls known as 'estreat' or extract rolls.
This again was probably done annually, but only a few such rolls
have survived for the two Earls Colne manors.

Only traces of the complex system of accounting have
survived for these two manors, but they support the view that
'nothing can be more carefully and more exhaustively drawn than the
bailiff's account' (Rogers 1909:54). The techniques of accounting
had grown out of the methods developed by the Royal Exchequer in
the twelfth century, when 'each estate had a series of annual
accounts modelled after those of the Crown' (Hone 1906:203). The
form of accounting was fully described in texts of the thirteenth
century, and did not change in its basic nature throughout the
period under consideration. Throughout they tended to be written in
Latin. Although the interspersing of totals within the text, rather
than at the end of the line, looks curious to us, it is unlikely
that an experienced bailiff or steward of the period would have
found it more difficult to deal with than any more recent system.
The grouping of items under various categories made it possible to
work out whether particular activities were making a profit or not,
and the making of profit was the one criterion put forward in all
the accounting treatises from the thirteenth century onwards. This
desire for profit, combined with the need for honesty, is

illustrated for example in the <u>Seneschaucy</u> (Oschinsky 1971:293) in
the early thirteenth century, where it is stated that the 'lord
ought to command and arrange that his accounts are audited every
year, not at one centre, but on each manor, for there one can learn
quickly the state of affairs and ascertain profit and loss'.

Diligent lords also kept their private accounts. We are
fortunate in Earls Colne to have two private account books. Similar
to the 'estreats' or extracts from court rolls is the book of
extracts of fines made by successive lords of the manor from 1610
onwards, for both of the two manors. These primarily record
admittances to copyhold properties and hence the fines paid at that
point. Much more general is the private account book kept by two
lords of the manor between 1603 and 1649. This is divided into
expenses and receipts, and includes many details concerning the
demesne, which are not available elsewhere. There are also numerous
personal notes of expenses and receipts.

Freehold property

There are three major sources of information on freehold property.
The first is deeds. 'Landowners of all kinds ... needed evidence of
their wealth in order to retain, exploit and transfer it. Above all,
they needed proof of possession, that is to say title deeds. Deeds -
 documents which recorded grants, sales, leases, agreements, and
settlements of disputes - form the basis of a landed society ...'
(Elton 1969:138-9). The many millions of such documents which were
produced in England from before the Norman Conquest up to the
eighteenth century may be roughly divided in two ways. There are
the original deeds and copies of such deeds, and there are those
documents which are in private hands and those in public
repositories. Roughly speaking, originals are in private hands and
copies in public institutions, but there are many exceptions to
this rule.

By far the largest quantity of deeds relating to Earls Colne
are in private hands, though temporarily deposited at the Essex

69

Record Office. These record the conveyance of the manors as well as individual properties within them. There is also a collection of deeds relating to the property of the grammar school and Quaker Meeting House in Earls Colne. They are often very lengthy documents, often written in Latin on parchment. Further deeds undoubtedly exist in private hands. Other deeds also exist in public collections. There are over 60,000 deeds in the Public Record Office, documents mostly deposited during law suits and never reclaimed (e.g. C.146-9, E.210, etc.). There are also tens of thousands of other deeds under 'additional charters' in the British Museum. These original deeds 'give an astonishing amount of information about land transactions' (Elton 1969:140). Yet, as the same author states, 'the evidence of copies is even more impressive'.

One major type of copy were collections known as 'cartularies', entry books of charters and deeds. Roughly 1,268 such cartularies written in England and Wales before 1485 have so far been found, over half of them are now deposited in the British Library. At least thirty of these were composed before 1200, and one of these was the cartulary of Colne Priory, containing 107 charters of the twelfth century, which has been published (Fisher 1946). The second major set of copies were those kept by the King's Chancery on the back of the 'close' rolls (C.54), extending from 1204 to 1903.

Deeds were instruments produced and executed by private individuals, with the advice of lawyers. A second major set of information concerning private land transactions were produced by a court, this is the class known variably as 'final concords', 'fines' or 'feet of fines'. They are deposited among the records of the court of Common Pleas (C.P.25). But the nature of these documents needs to be explained in more detail, since much of the detail is fictional and misleading at first sight.

A fine is a record of a final agreement, settlement or 'concord' in a common law action concerning land. The 'foot' is the record's triplicate copy, which was written at the lower end, or

70

'foot', of the parchment. Two copies were issued to those involved
in the case, and a third copy was kept by the court of Common Pleas
as a guarantee against forgery. They exist during a period of 650
years from 1182 to 1834 and were written in latin down to 1733,
except during the Commonwealth. The final agreement provided
someone with a king's court decision that he was the rightful
holder of certain land. The most normal type of action was one
where the deforciant or defendant was said to be forcibly excluding
the plaintiff from land which the plaintiff claimed that he owned.
But the matter is complicated by the fact that very soon the cases
became largely fictions. Latham writes that:

> The uses of this legal fiction were numerous. It could make a
> tenant secure by confirming his right and barring claims
> which might colourably be made to the land under the
> complicated medieval system of tenure. It could be a way of
> conveying land from one party to another ... Or it could be a
> method of providing for the inheritance of the land
> according to the present holder's wishes ... he might grant it
> nominally to one party, so that it could be granted, subject
> to some restriction, to another, or even back to himself
> (Latham 1952:7-8).

These final agreements, we are told, are 'often only one
necessary part of some wider transaction, and so can only be fully
understood with further evidence' (Latham 1952:8). They therefore
need to be integrated with private deeds in order to check the
accuracy of various pieces of information. The dates of the
documents are only approximately accurate, the holding was only
vaguely described and some of the description was inflated. The
area of land was 'only a rough approximation, if not an intentional
overstatement'. The value of the holdings can only be roughly
inferred from the 'consideration' recorded. Even the question of who
is conveying the holding to whom is sometimes unanswerable from the
document itself and Latham explains ways in which various fictions
are used to confuse this. Despite these complications, Latham
describes them as having 'a unique value as a repository of

71

information on the conveyance of freehold land over six and a half
centuries' (Latham 1952:9).

One of the central attractions of the final concords was that
'freehold property could not be passed or settled without expensive
licences from feudal lords and similar legal impediments' (Elton
1969:143), but by such a collusive action at common law a way was
found round this obstacle. It was harder for freeholders to avoid
paying another kind of fine, known as a 'relief'. The payment of such
reliefs leads to our third kind of record of freehold transfers.
Freeholds lay within certain manors and the owners were required to
do certain services and to pay certain reliefs to the lord of the
manor. The nature of the relief by the later period is well
described by Jacob (1741:10):

> Relief is a certain sum of money, which every freeholder
> payeth unto his lord, being at full age, at the death of his
> ancestor. It is the key, which opens the gate to give the heir
> free passage to the possession of his inheritance ... There is
> relief service, and relief custom - relief service is that
> which is paid upon the death of any freeholder; relief custom
> is that which is paid upon the death of any freeholder,
> change or alienation of any freehold, according to the custom
> of the place. In many places it is a year's profit of the
> lands, and in many other places but half a year's profit.

The reliefs which had to be paid were to be enrolled along with
copyhold transfers in the court roll. The reliefs were customarily
of a year's profits.

Copyhold property

The other major form of tenure was by tenants of the lord of the
manor who held under the rules of custom by way of a 'copy of court
roll' or copyhold. Certain customary lands could not be transferred
without the licence of the lord, usually upon the payment of a fine.

> If I will exchange a copyhold with another, I cannot do it by
> an ordinary exchange at the common law, but we must surrender
> to each other's use, and the Lord admits us accordingly. If I
> will devise a copyhold, I cannot do it by will at the common
> law, but I must surrender it to the use of my last will and

testament, and in my will I must declare my intent (Jacob
1741:6-7).
It might seem from this that the tenant was passing seisin or
possession over to the lord, and hence weakening his claim. But
Jacob stressed that this was not the case.

> A surrender (where by a subsequent admittance the grant is to
> receive its perfection and confirmation) is rather a
> manifesting the grantor's intentions, than of passing away
> any interest in the possession; for till the admittance the
> Lord taketh notice of the grantor as tenant, and he shall
> receive the profits of the lands to his own use, and shall
> discharge all services due to the Lord ... (Jacob 1741:6).

Here he was following earlier writers. Coke, for example, likened
the lord and his steward to a 'water-conduit' or 'instrument'
through whose hands the property flowed. At this stage, the lord
cannot interfere, nor can the grantee enter the premises, nor can
the grantor change his mind. The fact that the lord is merely
acting as a channel along which the possession moved is further
stressed under the question of admission: 'In voluntary admittances
the Lord is only esteemed custom's instrument ... And as in
admittances upon surrenders, so in admittances upon descents, the
Lord is used as a mere instrument, and no manner of interest
passeth out of him ...' (Jacob 1741:7). Hence it was the case that
'admittances by the Lord to a wrong person is void and of no effect
...'. From at least the fifteenth century, cases concerning copyhold
property could be brought to Chancery and by the 1570s or 1580s the
common law allowed the copyholder's lessee to bring an action of
ejectment (Baker 1979:260). Hence there was protection for the
copyholder not only in local custom but in equity and common law.
It is important to stress this fact since the wording of the actual
surrenders and admittances at first glance gives an impression of
far more power to the Lord than was indeed the case.

Most of the surrenders and admittances followed a fairly
simple formula, an example of which is given by Jacob (1741:41):

> I A.B. do surrender and yield up into the hands of W.A.Esq;
> Lord of this manor, all that messuage and tenement, with the

> appurtenances within this manor, now in the tenure of C.D. And
> all my estate, right, title, interest, possession, reversion,
> claim and demand whatsoever, of, in, and to the same, to the
> end the Lord may do therewith his will; and in token thereof
> I deliver up this virge [rod].

Usually there would be a short description of the property, but
this was often standardized and might not bear much relation to its
present nature. If the surrender was out of court, then witnesses
were named. Sometimes the surrender might be to the use of a man and
his wife and the longer lived of them, or to himself and a child, or
to the use of a will. It thus became possible to entail or tie up
the future of copyhold land. But descendants might wish to break
such entails and by about 1475 a legal fiction had been devised to
make it possible. This was known as a 'common recovery'. There are a
number of these in the Earls Colne manor court rolls and since they
are very misleading at first sight, being collusive or fictional
actions, it is necessary to explain this complex device. This is
best done in the words of a legal historian, John Baker (1979:235):

> In its simplest form, the alienee brought a real action
> against the alienor, the tenant in tail, on an imaginary
> title; the tenant called upon or 'vouched' a third party to
> warrant his title; the vouchee defaulted; and judgment was
> given for the alienee to recover the land. But for the
> voucher, the recovery could have been avoided ('falsified')
> by the issue in tail bringing actions of formedon. But the
> effect of the voucher was that the recoverer took an
> indefeasible title by the judgment, and the issue in tail
> were compensated by judgment against the defaulting vouchee
> for lands of equal value. The trick which was established by
> 1475 was for a humble, landless official of the court to lend
> his name (for a fee of 4d.) as the 'common vouchee'. The common
> vouchee would deliberately make default, and the issue would
> then be cut off with a worthless right to execute judgment
> against the lands of the landless defaulter.

After the tenant had made the surrender to the lord, he and
his heirs, or the person to whom he had conveyed it, were admitted.
In the example of A.B. already quoted, the steward would proceed to

re-admit A.B. with the following additions:

> Gentlemen of the Homage, you are to take notice, that the
> messuage and tenement, with the appurtenances now
> surrendered, is again granted to the said A.B. as sole
> purchaser ... to hold to him the said A.B. and C. and D. his
> sons, for the term of their lives, and the life of the longest
> liver of them successively, at the will of the Lord,
> according to the custom of this manor, by the yearly rent
> thereof of six shillings and eight pence, and by all other
> rents, charges, works, suits, customs and services therefore
> due, and of right accustomed. And for such estate so had in
> the premises, the said A.B. gives to the Lord for a fine forty
> pounds, in hand paid, or secured to be paid, and so he is
> admitted tenent thereof; and I do hereby give you seisin
> thereof (delivering him pen or rod) to hold the same
> accordingly (Jacob 1741:42).

The wording would naturally vary a little between manors and over
time, but the underlying features remained constant. If the heirs
or person to whom the holding was to be transferred failed to
appear in court to seek admittance, proclamation was to be made at
three courts for them to appear. If they failed to do so, or to send
someone with powers to act for them, then their possession reverted
to the lord. If the heir or grantee appeared and was successful in
seeking admittance, he had to swear an oath of fealty, which was not
recorded on the court rolls, as follows:

> You shall swear to become a true tenant to the honourable
> W.A.Esq; Lord of this manor, for the estate to which you are
> now admitted tenant. You shall from time to time bear, pay,
> and do all such rents, duties, services and customs therefore
> due, and of right accustomed. You shall from time to time be
> ordered and justified in all things at the Lord's courts, to
> be holden in and for the said manor of B. as other the tenants
> of the said manor, for their respective estates, are, shall,
> or ought to be; and you shall in all things demean yourself
> as a faithful tenant ought to do. So help you God (Jacob
> 1741:42-3).

The record of these transfers of land was first written out
in rough in court, as a draft of a court roll. A fair copy was then

made on parchment, a copy of each entry also being given to the
person admitted, this being his security and 'copy of court roll'.
Except for the brief period of the Interregnum, these transfers
were written in Latin on long parchment sheets which were then
rolled up. There are an average of about ten transfers a year in the
rolls for the manor of Earls Colne and about five a year for Colne
Priory. About 5,000 transfers have survived for the period before
1750, in which over 20,000 names appear. These transfers give us a
great amount of detailed information about the ownership of land
and houses and provide invaluable demographic, economic and social
data. They often fill in family relationships, give dates of death,
throw light on inheritance practices.

Court baron: customary jurisdiction

A manorial estate of necessity had to have a court baron; the
court baron 'is the chief prop and pillar of a manor, which no
sooner faileth, but the manor falleth to the ground.' (Coke 1764:49).
The holding of a court baron was a right which could not be created
by the sixteenth century, but could only be held on the basis of
ancient custom or 'prescription'. In essence, the court baron was a
court for civil actions between parties, where the Crown was not
involved. Analytically its functions can be divided in two, though
in practice they were inextricably mixed together both in the
sessions of the court and also in the record of the court on the
court roll. It is important to stress this fact, especially in
relation to the earlier period, since the schematic presentation in
this introduction tends to give a misleading impression of a rigid
division between the customary and common law jurisdiction of the
court baron. In the majority of courts it would be very difficult
to discern the differences. One part of its function stemmed from
its jurisdiction as a customary court, enforcing the particular and
local customs of a specific manor. In this, the only persons
concerned were the customary tenants and copyholders, and the lord
of the manor or his steward acted as judge. The main function was

Copyhold property

the taking and passing of estates, surrenders and admittances as
already described, and the court was usually held formally once or
twice a year for this purpose. Before it could be held, it was
necessary to have two customary tenants at least as suitors. But
the court also acted to prevent petty nuisances occurring on the
manor and to protect the lord's rights. The homage jury were to make
detailed enquiries concerning a number of matters. In the form of
the presentment jury, the homage was an active and very often the
predominant means by which offences were brought to manorial
courts in the area of customary jurisdiction. A manual on court
keeping gave the following charge to the court:

1 present all suitors owing suit
2 inquire concerning all tenants dead since the last court, what
   reliefs, wards etc. due to the lord
3 any right or service withdrawn from the lord
4 any bondman of blood that puts his son to school or sets him to
   craft or marries his daughter without leave
5 any bondman lets his land without leave or withdraweth his goods
   or chattels without leave
6 if lords commons are surcharged with animals
7 any bondman fled without fine or ransom
8 if any alienation of over twelve months and a day or lease for a
   term of years
9 any land changed from copyhold to freehold or vice versa which
   would disadvantage the lord
10 any cutting of the great timber
11 all trespassers, hunters or hawkers to be presented
12 any copyhold or other tenants let their tenements decay
13 any bondmen purchase free land without leave of the lord
14 any other things that ought to be presented
15 any make any rescues or break any arrest made by the bailiff
16 any remove road stones or stakes between tenants or lord
17 any tenant give land to the church without licence of the king
   and the lord

18 any encroachments on the lord's soil without licence
19 any holds two tenements and wasteth one and draws trees from one
    to the other etc.
20 any pull up trees or hedges, let houses fall down etc.
21 any keep or withdraw any evidences belonging to the lord, as
    court rolls etc. (Modus 1510:3-6; summarized and numbers added).

This general charge is largely the same as that in a model set of
instructions for holding a court baron compiled from courts held in
1434 (Roll 1434). With the omission of the articles about bondmen,
it is basically the same as that printed as a model by Jacob in the
early eighteenth century (Jacob 1741:36-8). Many matters arising
from these enquiries can be found in the court rolls of Earls Colne
and Colne Priory manors throughout the period, though they tend to
disappear in the second half of the seventeenth century.

    The exact nature of the procedure and punishments in this
court is not entirely clear. It appears that the homage would
present an offence, or an individual could bring a case against
another. The procedure was more like that of an equity court, and
could deal with minor matters which fell outside the common law.
Edward Coke claimed that

> In deciding controversies arising about the title of
> copyhold lands lying within his bounds: and when he sitteth
> as judge in court to end debates of this nature,he is not
> tied to the strict form of the Common law, and may redress
> matters in conscience upon bill exhibited, where the common
> law will afford no remedy in the same kind ... (Coke 1764:100).

> If a false judgment be given in a court baron by the Steward
> against a copyholder, the copyholder ... may sue in the court
> of the Lord by bill, to be relieved against such judgment; and
> the Lord, as Chancellor, may give him relief therein ... (Jacob
> 1741:18).

Thus it would appear that the procedure could follow that of the
bill and answer, rather than that of jury presentment and writ of
common law, and that the decision was taken by the lord or his
steward, and not by the homage jury, who made the presentment in

certain matters and stated the custom of the manor. It was in this
court that almost all real actions, those concerning copyhold land,
were to be tried. The one form of punishment that the customary
court could inflict was an 'amercement'. An amercement, or putting
someone in mercy, was a:

> pecuniary punishment for any offence committed by the tenant
> against the Lord of any manor. It is a certain sum of money
> imposed upon the tenant by the Steward, by the oath and
> presentment of the homage, for the breach of any bylaw ... or
> for default of doing suit, or for other misdemeanours,
> punishable by the same court (Jacob 1741:10-11).

It differed from a fine in that a person who was amerced could not
be lawfully imprisoned for non-payment. When an amercement was
granted a lord could enter an action of debt, or distrain from it,
and impound the distress and sell the object. The actual level of
the amercement was set by two to four 'affeerors' chosen by the
court.

Court baron: common law jurisdiction

The other major function of the court baron was as a court of
common law, the lowest rung on the ladder which led up through the
Quarter Sessions and <u>nisi prius</u> jurisdiction of the Assizes to the
courts of the King's Bench and Common Pleas. In terms of actions
which could be tried in the court, they were identical to those
'common pleas' tried at other common law courts. The particular
actions which Jacob singles out as likely to occur are as follows:
actions of debt, actions upon a case (a general action for redress
of wrongs done without force against any man, e.g. deceits, breaking
of contracts and bargains, etc.), slander, actions of trespass and
battery, actions of detinue, trover, etc. (i.e. recovery of goods or
things lent or delivered, recovery of damages to the value of them),
actions of waste (spoiling by a tenant for life or years) (Jacob
1741:249-342). One major condition upon which the actions could be
tried was that they were petty, involving sums of less than 40s.

The court was open to all freeholders or 'barons' residing

(or having real property in) the manor. It could only take place if
there were at least two suitors. It could be held every three weeks
and the freeholders being suitors were also the judges, less than
twelve being sufficient to act in this capacity. Since the
freeholders were the jury, the lord himself could bring an action
for himself against another, which he could not do in the court
leet where he or his steward was judge, or on the customary side of
the court baron. The procedure in court was in theory similar to
that of Quarter Sessions or other common law courts, and it could
therefore be as long and convoluted as that in, for example, Common
Pleas, with writs, warrants of attorney, answers, imparling,
replications, rejoinders, sur-rejoinders, rebutters, sur-rebutters,
etc.

 As far as punishments were concerned, the court did not have
the power to fine, that is to imprison for non-payment, but merely
to amerce, that is to distrain the defendant's goods and to retain
them until satisfaction was made. The damages which could be
claimed as a result of a successful plea are set out for the later
period by Jacob (1741:268) and vary between treble damages and
costs, and just damages.

Court leet

 For analytic purposes we may distinguish the court leet from
the 'view of frankpledge' and treat them separately, but it is
necessary to remember that, as Maitland argued concerning this
distinction and that between court baron and court leet, in
practice there was a great overlap.

> It is as we move towards modern times that a distinction
> between courts of various kinds becomes apparent; there is
> the court leet, the police court, exercising royal
> franchises, a court of record, in which, since it is the
> king's, jurors shall swear that they will keep the king's
> counsel and proclamation shall be made with a triple 'oyez!';
> suit to it is 'suit royal'; on the other hand is the court
> baron, a civil court, a court not of record, where no mention
> shall be made of the king's counsel and where only a single

'oyez!' is permissible; suit to it is 'suit service' (Maitland 1889:xviii).

Just as the common law side of the court baron could be seen as the lowest level of the chain of courts dealing with common pleas, leading up to the court of Common Pleas, so the court leet is the lowest level of the courts dealing with pleas of the Crown, above which stood the Justices of the Peace, Judges of Assize and King's Bench. Consequently a presentment at a court leet could be removed by <u>certiorari</u> into the court of King's Bench, where it could be traversed. Originally the word 'leet', an East Anglian word, seems to have meant a geographical division of the hundred. The country was divided up into areas and 'twice a year it was the sheriff's turn to hold these courts, and a court so holden by him came to be known as the sheriff's tourn. When such courts as these were in private hands, they were generally called courts leet' (Maitland 1919:46). The right to hold a court leet was thus a special franchise, anciently granted by charter or prescription (prescription is a custom relating to a specific individual). Thus only certain manors or boroughs or other greater franchises had a leet jurisdiction. The way in which the private leets fitted in with the royal leets is explained by Hearnshaw (1905:245)

> During the middle ages in fact, and in theory until the passing of the Sheriffs Act of 1887, every man in England and Wales lay within the precinct of some leet. For if he were not within the leet of any manor, municipality, or great franchise, then he was within the king's immediate leet, the sheriff's tourn.

But whereas the sheriff's tourn withered away before 1500 to be replaced by Commissions of the Peace and Justices of Assize, the private leets remained active in some areas until the eighteenth century. Thus the court leet is 'a court of record, ordained for punishing offences against the Crown; and is said to be the most ancient court of the land.' (Jacob 1744:s.v.court-leet).

The types of offence of which the court leet should take cognizance is indicated by the earliest printed 'charge of the leet', in 1510:

Here beginneth the charge of the leet

1 Present all headboroughs and their deceners that owe suit.

2 Also you shall inquire of petty treason if there be any among
  you that be money makers, or clippers, or wasters of the king's
  coin or counterfeiters of the king's seal or sleeth [cheateth]
  or deceiveth their masters ...

3 Also you shall inquire if there be any among you that putteth
  out any man's or woman's eye or cut out his tongue or cut his
  nose or disfiguring any member to the extent that they should
  not see or speak you shall do us to wete [know] thereof and of
  house burners and their recettours [receivers, harbourers].

4 Also if there be any small thieves among you that steal geese,
  capons, hens, chickens, shieves of corn in harvest or any other
  gear in men's windows prively that passeth not the value of xiii
  d.ob. [13-1/2d.] do us to wete thereof.

5 Also if there be any men among you that been receivers of
  thieves or that go in messages of felons as for vitail
  [victuals] or any other thing to their sustenance you shall do
  us to wete.

6 Also if you know among you any great thieves which steal meat,
  oxen, or kine, or sheep, or any other goods of great value ...

7 Any taken sanctuary and escaped without leaving the realm.

8 Any arrested for suspicion of felony and let go without any
  authority - their names.

9 Any forsworn king's land and returned again without special
  grace.

10 Any outlaws not pursued.

11 Also of all assaults and affrays made against the king's peace

12 Any rescued or arrests broken from the king's officers.

13 Also of all wounds made of blood shed or weapon drawn against
   the king's peace ...

14 Breakers of assize of bread.

15 All brewers and tapsters that keep not the assize and sell in

82

unsealed measures.

16 Any use double measures - i.e. a great measure to buy and a small measure to sell with.

17 All butchers, fishmongers and other victuallers who sell unwholesome food.

18 Any ditches, paths etc. unscoured and turned out of the right course.

19 All encroachments made upon public highways.

20 Any house, hedge or ditch or wall cast down, to the annoyance of the king's people.

21 Any 'white towers' [tawers] that sell not good merchandise and buy their skins in any other place than in town or markets.

22 All cordwayners and artificers who do not make good merchandise.

23 All those of 12 years old or more and have dwelt in the lordship twelve months and a day and be not sworn to the king ...

24 All persons who dispossess others, breakers that move stone stakes, and stealers of house doves.

25 Also of all common chiders and brawlers to the noyance of his neighbours and evesdroppers under men's walls or windows by night or by day to bear tales or to discover their counsel to make debate or dissension among their neighbours.

26 Any keeping a greyhound who cannot spend 40s. a year, or priest keeping a greyhound who cannot spend 10 pounds a year.

27 Any waifs of goods and chattels forfeit from felons.

28 Any stray animals come into the lordship.

29 Any purse cutters.

30 Any retailors or forestallers that lie in the way to buy corn or any other vitual at the towns end or in any other place to make the cheap [price] thereof dearer ...

31 Any miller taking excessive toll.

32 Any vagabonds or gamesters or robbers among you that wake on the night and sleep in the day and haunt the customable ale houses and taverns and routs about, and no man wotes [knows] from whence they come, nor whither they shall go ...

33 Any treasure found under the earth or above ground.

34 Any encroachments on king's possessions.

35 Also of all lollards if there be any among you and of their
   school you shall do us to wete.

36 Inquire of constable, aleconners, bailiffs and other officials
   to see if they have truly done their office.

37 All ravishers of women if there be any among you, their names.

38 Also of all manner of felonies and also robberies feloniously
   done within this lordship by whom, where, of what and what time
   if you find any such among you shall present it, etc.

39 Whether all defaults and complaints made on the last leet day
   were amended or not ... and of these points and of all other that
   you be wont to be charged of as for the court and for the leet
   that is worthy to be presented, you shall go together and bring
   in true verdict (Modus 1510:6-12; summarized, partly modernized
   and numbers added).

A comparison of this summary of the charge to the leet in
1510 with the model charge in 1434 (Roll 1434) shows a great deal
of similarity, and often identical wording, even the order is
substantially the same. But a comparison of the 1510 edition to the
1650 edition of a similar manual shows how much had been added to
the duties of the court leet. Although the court leet was 'rigidly
limited to its common law powers' and could 'only take cognizance of
the newer statutory offences if it had been given power to do so by
the statute which created the offence' (Holdsworth 1966:136), many
of the statutes of the sixteenth and seventeenth centuries which
extended the power of Justices of the Peace also empowered the
court leet to act. Thus the 1650 edition lists and defines
twenty-eight major offences which were to be enquired of, including
all the normal felonies such as clipping and coining, homicide,
manslaughter, rape, burglary, robbery, etc., which 'are to be
enquired of, and presented in court leet, but not punishable there'
(Order 1650:10). The following matters, not mentioned in the 1510
edition, had been added to the list of matters to be presented in

the leet and to be punished there:

8 If any laystalls be made, or any carrion be cast in highways, to the annoyance of the people, this is enquirable.

16 If any keep and maintain any bawdery in their houses, it is cause of breaking the peace, and it is a vice that corrupteth the Commonweal, and for that cause it is here to be enquired of.

18 Also if there be any that be common haunters of taverns or alehouses, having not sufficient to live upon, they are to be enquired of.

20 Also you shall enquire if any person have watered any hemp or flax in any river, running water stream or brook, or other common pond where beasts do use to drink ...

26 Also that hostlers do not sell hay, nor oats but at reasonable prices, and that they do not take for the bushell, but an half penny over the common price in the market, and that they take nothing for the litter, and this is enquirable.

27 An innkeeper may bake his bread for horses in his house in any throughfare town which is no city where no common bakers dwell, and if he bake and not make the same according to the prices of grain, it is to be punished in leet.

33 Also the constable ought to see the peace and watch to be observed as it ought.

38 If any horse or mare be put upon a waste ground, and be scabbed, or having an infectious disease, he shall forfeit to the Lord of the leet ten shillings, and this is enquirable.

39 If any exigent be awarded against one indicted of felony, by the keeping of his goods, they are forfeit, though after he be acquitted of felony, and the Lord by charter shall have his goods, and not by prescription , and this is enquirable.

40 If any be outlawed in debt, trespass or other personal action, his goods be forfeited, and the Lord shall have them by charter, and not by prescription, and this is enquirable.

41 Also you shall enquire if the common fine be here paid according to the custom, and whether the same be gathered according unto

the usage ...

42 Note that every one that hath view of free pledges, ought to have pillory and tumbrell to do justice: also in every town where there is a leet, there shall be stocks, and for default thereof, the town shall forfeit five pound, and the same is enquirable.

43 Also you shall enquire whether any have used in any of their garments, velvet, sattin, damask, taffata, sarcenet, chamlet: or any fur, as foins, lennets, martins, squirril, fox, gray, cony, hare, or other furres growing within this land; or gold, or silver, in or upon any of their garments, otherwise than the Statutes made in the 14 yeare H.8 and 1. and 2. of Ph. and Mary do allow, you shall present the offenders.

44 Also you shall enquire whether any baker, brewer, butcher, cook, tipler, &c. do take excessive gain or no: also whether they conspire, covenant, promise, or take an oath not to sell victuall but at a certain price, & present the same.

45 The same for artificers, workmen, or labourers in relation to work at certain prices.

46 Any tanner selling any hide gashed or cut, twelvepence per hide fine.

47 Also no currier ought to curry any leather in a shoemaker's house: and none ought to curry any leather evil tanned.

48 Also you shall enquire if there be any crow nets, if there be not, the Lord shall have the moity of ten shillings, which shall be forfeited by the parish or town for not having the same. Also if they destroy not the crow nests when they begin to breed, they shall be amerced.

49 Also you shall enquire if any person by any means hath taken and killed any young brood, spawn or fry of salmons, eels, pikes, or any other fish, in any stream, river, brook, floodgate, or in the tail of any mill, and present the offenders. And further, when any person hath taken in any of the places aforesaid, any salmons or trouts out of season, or pikes, or pikrels, not being in length ten inches, or any barbel not being in length twelve

inches, or any salmons not sixteen inches, or trouts not eight
inches long: if any have done so, they shall forfeit certain
penalties.

50 Any broken the head of any pond or pool with fish in with intent
to destroy them - penalty of three months and sureties for
seven years good behaviour.

52 Also you shall enquire if any person do keep or maintain any
common house, alley or place of bowling, quoits, cailes, tennis,
dicing, tables, or carding, or any other unlawful games - also if
any haunt such places.

53 No stoned horse being of the age of two years, except he be
fourteen hands high, shall be put to pasture in any common ... any
mare, foal or gelding, not likely to be able to bear foals, or to
do profitable service, the same shall be slain and buried.

54 Also you shall enquire if the inhabitants after robberies and
felonies committed, do make fresh suit from town to town, or from
county to county, or from hundred to hundred according to the
Statute of Winchester 13.E.1.cap.2. For if a man be robbed in the
day time, and the thief escape, and is not taken within forty
days after the robbery, for lack of hue and cry, the borough or
hundred shall answer to the party all his goods and damages:
also if any person be killed in a town in the day time, and the
murderer or manslayer escape not taken or arrested by those of
the town, then the township shall be amerced. 18.Ed.2.

55 Constables and church-wardens to appoint surveyor of the
highways, anyone refusing to do so pay 20s; has surveyor done his
job.

56 Ditches scoured and bushes cut, according to Statute of 1 Eliz.

57 Half of the forfeitures for these statutes, the church-wardens
to have to bestow upon high-ways.

59 Also you shall enquire whether any refuse to come to musters
before any person authorized to take the same, he shall be
imprisoned for ten days, except he pay 40s, and if any persons
appointed to take musters, receive any money to release any

appointed to serve, he shall forfeit ten times so much as that
he received. 4 & 5 P & M,ca.3.

60 If any persons to the number of twelve make an unlawful
assembly, for to break any banks, inclosures, parks, fish-ponds,
barns, houses, and such like ... every such attempt is felony ...
people to assist law officers in suppressing and not to assist
rioters ...

61 None may trace, destroy or kill a leveret in the snow with a dog
...

62 Also you shall enquire if those persons, which do sell wines be
thereunto licensed. ...

An addition of divers other matters enquirable in leets, not
mentioned in the former edition.

1 It is lawful to all stewards and bayliffs in their several leets
and law-days, to enquire, hear and determine every offence
committed contrary to the tenure of the Statute made 33 H.8.
concerning cross-bows and hand-guns ...

2 And if any jury sworn and charged to enquire of any offences
committed contrary to the said statute, do wilfully conceal any
of the said offences: then the stewards or bailiffs before whom
any concealment shall be had, have authority to charge and swear
another jury of twelve or more, to enquire of such concealment
...

4 Lords in leets, and their stewards within the precinct of their
leets, have authority to enquire and take presentment by oath of
jurors, of all and every offence and offences committed contrary
to the Statute 31 Eliz. touching the erecting and maintaining of
cottages and inmates ...

5 Stewards may enquire concerning an act Eliz. 6 for the
preservation of pheasants and partridges (Order 1650:15-30;
summarized and modernized).

Even if only some of these matters were presented and
punished, it can be seen how important the court leet was in the
policing of the village. This raises the important question of the

degree of the discrepancy between the theory and practice. In his
study of the Southampton Court Leet, Hearnshaw was led to remark
that 'It would be difficult to invent, or even to conceive, a body
of entries less like the model presentments of the court keepers'
guides ...' (Hearnshaw 1905:198). Only a detailed study of a
particular leet court will enable us to establish whether this was
the case there.

As regards the meetings, we are told that the court leet 'by
the statute of Magna Charta is to be kept but twice every year;
within a month after Easter and another time within a month after
Michaelmas' (Coke 1764:50). Its procedure was basically similar to
that of the Justices at the Quarter Sessions or the Assizes: 'The
sheriff or the steward ... addressed a list of questions known as
the "articles of the tourn" to the representatives of the various
townships in the hundred just as the royal justices in eyre
addressed articles of the eyre to the various bodies representing
the county ...' (Radcliff and Cross 1954:74). In both the sheriff's
tourn and the court leet the business 'is transacted by means of
presentments and indictments preferred by a jury' (Maitland
1889:xxvii). The lord or his steward was the judge.

A thirteenth-century manuscript, which is significantly
entitled 'Le Court de Baron', even though it is dealing with what we
would later classify as court leet business, gives an interesting
idea of the earlier procedures (Hone 1906:132-40). In one case, the
bailiff complains to the steward, and the court awards compurgation
with five neighbours to acquit the person of the charge. Such a
method with compurgation was later only used by the ecclesiastical
courts. In two more serious cases of horse stealing and burglary,
the procedure appears to be very similar to that in the other
common law courts. In the first case the bailiff calls for the
prisoners to be brought before him, and asks what is the charge. He
cross-questions the prisoner, who answers. The bailiff suggests
that 'thou canst right boldly put thyself upon the good folk of
this vill that thou didst not steal her'. The prisoner replies that

89

the neighbours believe evil reports of him and would not do him
justice, to which the bailiff amswers that 'thou canst oust from
among them all those thou suspectest of desiring condemnation ...',
after which the accused confesses his crime. In the second case, the
accused denies the charge and asks that 'I put myself upon the jury
of the vill for good and for ill', and it is ordered that 'an inquest
be made'. Thus it would appear that in small cases there might be
summary sentence or compurgation, while in more complex and serious
cases normal common law procedures were to be followed.

The important role of the jury or 'inquest' as it was called
in the 1510 edition is shown by the oath they had to take upon the
Holy Sacrament:

> Thou shalt truly inquire and true presentment make of all
> that thou shalt be charged of in the king's behalf, and of the
> lords of this franchise, this worthy to be presented, that is
> for to say the king's counsell, thy fellows and thine own will
> and truly keep and for nothing let, but say so help thee God
> and thy holy dome (sacrament) and bid him kiss the book ...
> (Modus 1510:2; modernized).

The oaths were even more elaborate in the 1650 edition, that of the
foreman ending with the words: 'but you shall present and tell the
truth, the whole truth, and nothing but the truth, so help you God,
and by the contents of this Book. And this being done, cause him to
kiss the Book' (1650:4). After each individual juryman had taken a
separate oath, the 1650 edition (5-10) spends four and a half pages
outlining an 'exhortation to be given unto the Jury before the
charge, to consider their oath', in which they were exhorted by all
that was sacred and holy to make a true presentment. The jury in a
court leet must consist of at least twelve persons, whereas that of
a court baron could consist of less than twelve; 'the reason of that
is, because none are impanelled upon the jury in courts-barons but
freeholders of the same manor, but in court-leets strangers are
sometimes impanelled' (Coke 1764:51). The powers of the court leet
were generally limited. Those cases 'which are to be punished with
loss of life or member, are only inquirable and presentable here,

Copyhold property

and to be certified over to the Justices of Assize.Stat.1.Ed.3.'
(Jacob 1744:s.v.court-leet). Thus it could not punish felonies, only
misdemeanours. Jacob continued that

> a court leet may fine, but not imprison: a steward may impose
> a reasonable fine, for a contempt in court; or commit those
> who make an affray before him, in the execution of his office,
> or bind them to the peace or good behaviour: but he may not
> grant surety of the peace, unless by prescription...The usual
> method of punishment in the court leet, is by fine and
> amercement; the former assessed by the steward, and the
> latter by the jury: for both of which, the lord may have an
> action of debt, or take a distress, &c.

The lord of the leet 'ought to have a pillory and tumbrel to punish
offenders ... Also all towns in the leet are to have stocks in
repair ...' (Jacob 1744:s.v.court-leet). Clearly, therefore, some
forms of minor physical discomfort could be used as punishments.
The steward and court leet also had the power to elect officers,
such as constables and tithing-men, to carry out their duties. As
with the court baron, the court would select between two and four
'affeerors', who were to assess the level of fines and amercements.

Both of the two manors in Earls Colne had the extra franchise
of a court leet. The court rolls therefore contain numerous court
leet presentments, for the courts leet remained active until about
1620. On average, between twenty and thirty cases a year were
presented in the two courts combined. Allowing for the loss of some
of the rolls, we can estimate that roughly three or four thousand
court leet cases of one kind or another survive for this parish.

View of frankpledge

Maitland argued that the word 'leet' is of late invention and
that before the thirteenth century, the court was called more often
the 'view of frankpledge', or, in other words, the inspection of the
free pledges. There is, therefore, no real distinction between view
of frankpledge and court leet (Maitland 1889:xvi-xix). This theory
is anticipated by Jacob in the eighteenth century when he writes
that the court leet 'is called the View of Frankpledge'. This was

91

'because the King is to be there certified by the View of the
Steward, how many people are within every leet, and have an account
of their good manners and government' (Jacob 1744:s.v. court-leet).

Without going into the dispute over the origins of the
system, what is clear is that by 1400 the frankpledge was
flourishing, and where a court leet had been granted to a
particular lordship or estate the lord had the right to hold a view
of frankpledge. In theory the view was to ensure that 'every person
of the age of 12 years, which hath remained there for a year and a
day may be sworn to be faithful to the King' (Jacob 1744:s.v.
court-leet).

In theory, all those aged from twelve to sixty years of age
who dwelt within the leet were obliged to do suit of court, except
peers and clergymen, unless they were under the sheriff's tourn.
Handbooks stressed this duty and gave a model of the oath of
allegiance which each person had to take once or twice a year when
the view was held.

> I shall true liege man be and true faith bear to King Henry
> the Seventh that now is and to his heirs and be no thief nor
> thieves companion, nor thief know, nor treason, nor keep it
> counsel but I shall inform and do to know them that be the
> King's officers that have the law in governance, etc. And
> shall be compliant and obedient to the justices and
> commissioners, sherrifs escheatours bailiffs and constables
> and to all other officers of the King in all that they shall
> charge me lawfully, so help me God, etc. (Modus 1510:24-5;
> modernized).

If such a system had been extensive, with personal appearance of
most of the adult males twice a year, the swearing of oaths of
allegiance and presentment of defaulters, it would clearly be of
the utmost importance in instilling a sense of the national law.

In practice the thoroughness of the views varied both
between manors and over time. An analysis of the views in Earls
Colne suggested that in the late Elizabethan period, the views
provide 'a good coverage of a large proportion of adult males'

(Macfarlane 1976:126). But in the fifteenth and early sixteenth centuries there are periods when the lists are much shorter, perhaps only naming the chief pledges. In the manor of Earls Colne there are such views over most of the period 1400-1700, while in Colne Priory manor views have been sporadically recorded between 1490 and about 1700. Allowing for the loss of records, this parish produced roughly between 20,000 and 30,000 names in the views of frankpledge over the whole period up to 1750. The names are written in lists at the start of each session of the court, on the court rolls, often indicating those who had 'essoined' or put in excuses for absence, and noting the fines to be paid by those who had failed to appear and made no essoin.

> One other franchise needs to be mentioned. As Maitland wrote
> The lord who has the view of frankpledge usually has also the
> 'assize of beer', that is, the power of enforcing the general
> ordinances which from time to time fix the prices at which
> beer may be sold; sometimes, but much more rarely, he claims
> the assize of bread. Out of beer the lords made some
> considerable profit (Pollock and Maitland 1968:581-2).

In both Earls Colne and Colne Priory, the lord had both assizes of bread and ale and this led to many presentments.

Conclusion

Despite the loss of a number of court rolls, rentals, account rolls and other documents, and despite the fact that we have only the fair copies in most cases, the records created by the holders of estates in Earls Colne constitute a very large archive. For Earls Colne the records are considerably larger in quantity than the records produced by the Church and by the State combined. This was not only the result of the importance of land holding, but also because the 'estate' or manor was much more than just a landholding institution. The four functions it performed are summarized by Maitland: 'Thus we may regard the typical manor (1) as being, qua vill, an unit of public law, of police and fiscal law, (2) as being an unit in the system of agriculture, (3) as being an unit in the

93

management of property, (4) as being a jurisdictional unit'
(Pollock and Maitland 1968:597). All the specific records discussed
here for Earls Colne, with the exceptions of some of the deeds and
feet of fines at the Public Record Office and British Library, are
on deposit at the Essex Record Office.

5. Ecclesiastical jurisdiction

The officials and bodies which compiled the mountain of paper which
recorded the major activities of the Church were generally
speaking located at four levels of a hierarchical structure. This
was the case throughout England. In order to provide a concrete
example of how this worked we shall describe the system in Essex
and specifically the Archdeaconry of Colchester within which Earls
Colne was located. As we have earlier stressed, those working on
other areas will need to modify this account somewhat since each
jurisdiction had its own idiosyncrasies. At the level of the parish
there was the incumbent, helped by churchwardens and overseers of
the poor, or other officials such as sidesmen. In Earls Colne the
next significant level up was the Archdeaconry of Colchester, for
the Deanery of Lexden does not seem to have been a record-producing
body during this period, or at least no records are known to have
survived. The bishopric was in theory above the archdeaconry. In
practice they had coterminous jurisdiction, though there were
rights of appeal upwards. In our case there was the Bishop of
London who exercised his power principally through two courts, the
Consistory and his Commissary in Essex and Hertfordshire. At the
top level there was the Archbishop of Canterbury. Thus of our seven
types of record, the parish produced the registers and the poor
administration documents and had some part in producing accounts
of church administration, while the archdeaconry and bishopric
produced or stored the other records.

95

Ecclesiastical jurisdiction

The jurisdictional boundary between the bottom level and the archdeaconry is clear, but it is necessary to say a little more about the relations between Archdeacon, Consistory and Commissary. Richard Burn described the relationship between the archdeacon and bishop as follows:

> By the canon law the archdeacon is styled the bishop's eye; and hath power to hold visitations (when the bishop is not there); and hath also power under the bishop of the examination of clerks to be ordained, as also of institution and induction; likewise of excommunication, injunction of penances, suspension, correction, inspecting and reforming irregularities and abuses among the clergy; and a charge of the parochial churches within the diocese: in a word, according to the practice of, a latitude given by the canon law, to supply the bishop's room, and (as the words of that law are) in all things to be the bishop's vicegerent ⌈sic⌉ (Burn 1788A:i,89).

Burn then added that 'By the statute of the 24 H.8.c.12. an appeal lieth from the archdeacon's to the bishop's court.' He also cited a case which suggested that except where the archdeacon has a peculiar or special jurisdiction: 'then the bishop and he have concurrent jurisdiction and the party may commence his suit, either in the archdeacon's court or the bishop's, and he hath election to choose which he pleaseth' (Burn 1788A:i,89-90). We can see from this the overlap between the levels and it is further shown in Burn's definition of the two branches of the bishop's powers, his Consistory and Commissary. Under 'Consistory' Burn wrote :

> Consistory is the court christian, or spiritual court, held formerly in the nave of the cathedral church ... in which the bishop presided... But this court now is held by the bishop's chancellor or commissary, and by archdeacons or their officials, either in the cathedral church or other convenient place of the diocese, for the hearing and determining of matters and causes of ecclesiastical cognizance, happening within that diocese (Burn 1788A:ii,11).

Thus we see that the bishop's power was exercised simultaneously in his own Consistory, through his chancellor, and by his Commissary

and by the archdeacons. The relevant Commissary for Earls Colne was
the Bishop of London's Commissary in Essex and Hertfordshire who
acted for the bishop throughout the county of Essex. Burn described
the literal meaning of 'Commissary' as follows: 'Commissary is a
title of jurisdiction, appertaining to him that exerciseth
eccesiastical jurisdiction in places of the diocese so far distant
from the chief city, that the chancellor cannot call the people to
the bishop's principal Consistory Court without great trouble to
them' (Burn 1788A:ii,7). Burn continues by pointing out that the
Commissary was particularly important in the parishes exempt from
the archdeacon's jurisdiction. In theory, individuals from Earls
Colne could be cited and could start their cases, as well as appeal,
to the Commissary.

     Two other ecclesiastical courts also had superior
jurisdictions over the inhabitants of Earls Colne. One was the
Archbishop's Court, known as the Court of Arches. Unfortunately,
most of the medieval records were destroyed in the Great Fire of
London and there are few records for the period before 1660. A
search of the surviving earlier records at Lambeth Palace and those
for 1660 onwards indexed by Jane Houston did not reveal any Earls
Colne cases and only a handful for Essex (Houston 1972). A search
of the other archives at Lambeth revealed no court records, and
only one or two administrative records, relating to this parish.

     The other potential source was the Court of High Commission
which was set up as a result of the royal supremacy over the Church
established at the Reformation and institutionalized in the later
seventeenth century. The detailed records which have survived for
the northern branch of the Commission at York suggests that a
number of Essex cases would have been found. The court had a
concurrent jurisdiction with the bishop's courts. The records for
Canterbury were destroyed when the institution was abolished in
1640, but one occasionally finds a volume in diocesan archives. It
is also worth mentioning the High Court of Delegates whose records
are now at the Public Record Office in Chancery Lane.

Ecclesiastical jurisdiction

We have seen the physical jurisdiction of the various
authorities, but we also have to consider the nature of the matters
which were of ecclesiastical concern. The very wide area covered by
the ecclesiastical courts is best demonstrated by the specific
example of a set of visitation articles. While it is true that they
were particularly lengthy and detailed as a result of Archbishop
Laud's attempt to reform the Church, most of the topics covered are
to be found in other episcopal and archidiaconal articles. Since
they are so lengthy, we will summarize most of the articles
(Articles 1635).

Articles to be enquired of within the Archdeaconry of
Colchester, 1635
Articles concerning the clergy.

1 Does the minister read the constitutions once a year?
2 Does the minister pray for King and Queen?
3 Does the minister observe divine service and other prescribed
rites?
4 Does the minister administer holy communion so each may receive
three times a year?
5 Does the minister admit notorious offenders or schismatics to
the communion?
6 Does the minister ensure that parishioners take communion three
times a year?
7 Does the minister sign those being baptized with the sign of the
cross?
8 Is the minister continually resident upon his benefice?
9 Does the minister, if he is a preacher, usually preach?
10 Is the minister licensed to preach; if not, does he procure a
preacher?
11 Has the minister another benefice?
12 Is the curate licensed?
13 If the minister is not licensed to preach, does he read the

homilies?

14 Are any allowed to preach in your church, except those known to be licensed?

15 Does the lecturer or preacher personally read the service twice a year at least?

16 Does the minister wear a surplice while saying public prayer?

17 Does the minister instruct the youth and ignorant persons in catechism, articles, etc.?

18 Does the minister solemnize irregular marriages without a licence?

19 Does the minister solemnize marriage of those under 21 years without parental consent?

20 Does the minister warn parishioners of Holy Days and Fasting days?

21 Does the minister perambulate the parish on rogation days?

22 Does any man, not a minister, practice any clerical duties in the church?

23 Does the minister every six months denounce in church all excommunicate persons?

24 Does the minister try to reclaim papists?

25 Is the minister 'over-conversant' with papists?

26 Does the minister or anyone else carry out a rite in a private house?

27 Does the minister or any other carry out a fast or prophecy not approved or established?

28 Does anyone hold private meetings or 'conventicles' in their house?

29 Does the minister wear decent apparel for services?

30 If any former minister or deacons have become lay-men, what are their names?

31 'Whether is your minister noted or defamed to have obtained his benefice by simony, or reputed to be an incontinent person, or doth keep any man or woman in his house, that are suspected either to be of evil religion, or bad life, himself to be a

common drunkard, or to be a common haunter of taverns, alehouses, or other suspected places, a common gamester, or player at dice, or other unlawful games, a common swearer, or notorious person ... ?'

32 Does the minister perform thanksgiving of women after their child-birth and does he admit without licence any to that rite who were begotten in fornication or adultery?

33 Are any baptized in any vessel other than the font?

34 Does the minister keep any excommunications in his custody for more than twenty days without publishing them?

35 Does the minister receive any excommunicate persons to communion without a certificate of absolution?

36 Has the minister absolved any persons without a special warrant?

37 Does the minister read the divine service on the various specified festivals?

Articles concerning the church.

1 Is there a Book of the Canons Ecclesiastical in the church?

2 Is there a parchment register book for baptisms, marriages and burials?

3 Is there a Book of Common Prayer, font, communion table, linen cloth, table of the Ten Commandments, in the church?

4 Is there a seat for the minister, a pulpit, suplice, communion cup of silver, strong chest for the alms for the poor and chest for ornaments?

5 How many bells are there and are there other church goods missing?

6 Are the church house, the church, the churchyard all in good repair?

7 Do any withold any church stock or church goods given for charitable uses?

Articles concerning schoolmasters.

Ecclesiastical jurisdiction

1 Is any schoolmaster of good religion, sound teaching and
licensed?

2 Does the schoolmaster receive communion and cause his pupils to
do so?

3 Does the schoolmaster teach catechism?

4 Does the schoolmaster privately instruct in superstition,
disobedience, etc.?

5 Are there any papists, and do they keep any schoolmasters?

6 Does any schoolmaster teach grammar other than the 'King's
Grammar'?

Articles concerning the parishioners, and others of the laity.

1 Do any impugn the King's supremacy and authority in
ecclesiastical causes?

2 Do any deny the Church of England to be the true church?

3 Do any impugn the Articles of Religion of 1562?

4 Do any impugn the rites and ceremonies of the Church of England?

5 Do any impugn the government of the Church of England?

6 Do any impugn the form of consecration of officers of the Church
of England?

7 Do any hold or attend private meetings or 'conventicles'?

8 Do any drink publicly or work on Sundays or other holy days?

9 Have any profaned the Lord's Day?

10 Have any struck or quarrelled with the minister or any other in
the church or churchyard or used filthy or immodest behaviour
there?

11 Do all use reverence and humility in the time of divine service?

12 Do churchwardens and others search for those absent from church?

13 Is there a sufficient quantity of bread and wine?

14 Are there any who act as godparents to their own children; do
godparents use the proper answers as in the Book of Common
Prayer; are any excommunicate persons made godparents?

15 Do any refuse to have children baptised, or refuse to receive

101

communion because the minister is not a preacher?

16 Do parents and masters cause children and servants to be catechised?

17 Do any pardons, plays, feasts, banquets, church-ales, drinking occur in the church or churchyard?

18 How many inhabitants over the age of fifteen refuse to attend church or communion?

19 Do any entertain guests or lodgers who refuse to attend church or communion?

20 Are there papists of insolent behaviour or who instruct children in popish religion?

21 How long have papists abstained from divine service and communion?

22 What are the names of all excommunicated persons in the parish?

23 How have the churchwardens been chosen; have previous churchwardens given in their accounts?

24 Do all parishioners over the age of sixteen attend divine service and communion?

25 Is there a fit parish clerk aged over twenty?

26 Is the church clean and the doors locked?

27 Have any been married within the prohibited degrees?

28 Do any divorced or already married persons keep company as man and wife with another?

29 'Whether have you in your parish, to your knowledge, or common fame and report, any who have committed adultery, fornication, or incest, or any bawds, harbourers or receivers of such persons, or publicly suspected thereof, which have not been publicly punished to your knowledge? ... any reputed common drunkards, blasphemers of God's holy name, common and usual swearers, filthy speakers, railers, sowers of discord among their neighbours, or speakers against minister's marriages, usurers contary to the Statute 37 Henry VIII, simonical persons, fighters, brawlers or quarrelers in the church or churchyard? You shall not fail to present their names.'

30 Are there any harbourers of women begotten with child out of
wedlock?

31 Are there any suspected of incontinency who have left the parish
and then returned?

32 Does anyone keep libellous books, especially concerning
Catholicism?

33 Does anyone keep mass books, breviaries, copes, vestments, etc.?

34 Are any absent from sermons, or go to sermons in other parishes?

35 Do any inn-keepers, ale-wives or others suffer gaming or
drinking during sermons; are there any fairs or markets on
Sundays in the churchyard?

36 Does any minister without permission cause a person to be
punished or fined for an offence of an ecclesiastical kind?

37 Do any come only to the sermons and not the rest of the service;
do any refuse to kneel or wear their hats during the service?

38 Do any refuse to come to church after a child-birth to give
thanks in fit apparel?

39 Do any resort to private meetings or 'conventicles'?

40 Do any keep children unbaptized longer than is necessary or take
them to be baptized elsewhere?

41 Do any meddle with the goods of deceased persons without
permission?

42 What are the names of those who do not attend the holy
communion?

43 Is there any other matter of ecclesiastical cognizance that
should be presented?

44 Do people keep as Holy Days the prescribed festivals as the
Birth of Jesus, etc.?

45 Is the 5th of November kept holy and thanksgiving given to God?

46 Churchwardens are to provide a sheet and white wand to be kept
in church and used in the punishment of offenders.

Even in this highly abridged form, it can be seen how minute
was the enquiry into a parish's spiritual and moral life. In this
particular case there are several further articles, mainly

concerning the prosecution of Roman Catholics, based upon the
directions of the Privy Council. The burden on the churchwardens
and 'sworn-men' was clearly very considerable. They were therefore
required to take the following oath, appended to the articles:

> you shall swear, that all affection, hatred, hope of reward,
> or gain, or fear of displeasure or malice set aside, you shall
> upon due consideration of the articles given you in charge,
> present to the arch-deacon of Colchester, or his official,
> all and every such person within your parish as hath
> committed any offence, or fault, or made any default
> mentioned in any of these articles, or which are vehemently
> suspected, or otherwise defamed of any such offence, fault, or
> default, wherein you shall deal uprightly, and according to
> equity, neither of malice presenting any contrary to truth,
> nor of corrupt affection sparing to present any, and to
> conceal the truth, having in this action God before your
> eyes, with an earnest zeal to maintain truth, and to supress
> vice: so help you God, and his faithful promises in Christ
> Jesus. God Save the King.

Records of church administration and finance
The vast and complex ecclesiastical organization of the church, one
of the major landowners and employers in the country, required a
great deal of administration. The records which this generated are
voluminous and we will both simplify and omit a great deal in this
description. We will concentrate on four functions which have left
records: the ordination of the clergy, the inspection of clergy and
other church officials, the inspection of church movable property
and buildings, and the surveying of other immovable property in the
shape of lands and rents.

The parish church of St Andrews in Earls Colne was originally
a rectory and there remained a rector throughout. But in 1355 the
prior of Colne made an agreement whereby a vicar was established.
The Priory continued as patron of the living until the suppression
in 1534 when the patronage passed into the hands of the Earls of
Oxford. There was later a dispute over the right of presentation,
but it then passed into the hands of the Harlakenden family and

their heirs. The presentations to livings and ordination registers
of the Bishops of London have been searched by Newcourt, and he has
listed the vicars (Newcourt 1710:ii, 185-6). The names of later
vicars, churchwardens and sidesmen also appear in various
'visitation' records. When a new Bishop of London was installed he
would either in person or by a deputy make a visitation of the
whole bishopric. Thereafter, there were visitations every three
years. Vicars and other ecclesiastical officials had to appear
personally and be examined.

The records of the Bishop of London's Commissary are again
divided. At the Guildhall there are churchwardens' presentments
(Ms. 9583), visitation books (Ms. 9537) and visitation processes
(Ms. 9583A). A search of all these records between 1554 and 1750 led
to the discovery of some Earls Colne presentments. At the Essex
Record Office there are three volumes of visitations to 1725
(D/ABV). Also at the Essex Record Office are two volumes of
visitations between 1625 and 1639 at the Bishop of London's
Consistory (D/ALV). Finally, the Archdeacon of Colchester also made
visitations and there are eighteen volumes between 1586 and 1750
(D/ACV).

These visitations had a second function, which was to check
the general state of repair of the movable property and buildings
of the church. Thus in some of the more detailed visitations, and in
the presentments which often arose out of them, we find concern
over church fabric, furniture, ornaments, bells, plate, the upkeep
of churchyards and fences, the provision and condition of bibles,
books of common prayer and parish registers. Most of these matters
are touched on in the Earls Colne visitation and ex officio
records.

The financing of the church was a major preoccupation of the
officials. In Earls Colne we are able to investigate the sources of
such financing in unusual detail through the diary and accounts of
one of the vicars, Ralph Josselin (Macfarlane 1970:34-7). In 1650
some parliamentary surveyors put the value of the living at £24,

plus £4 a year from glebe land. In fact, from private contributions
and elsewhere, Josselin at this time believed he was obtaining
about £60 per annum. This was supplemented by about £20 per annum
when, in 1659 informally, and from 1673 by formal deed, the great
tithes were given to the vicars by the rector, Richard Harlakenden.
The actual physical property was described in a terrier of 1610 as
'A mansion or vicarage-house, with stable and out-houses, and a
dove-house, much decayed, with gardens and yards adjoining,
containing one acre; also, one acre and one rood more of glebe'
(Newcourt 1710:ii,185).

Mere office or summary correction records

Over three-quarters of the material for Earls Colne in the
ecclesiastical courts falls within this category. The proceedings
were concerned with causes of correction instituted on the basis of
the mere office of the judge (ex officio mero), and consequently
the start of each presentment contains the phrase 'the office of
the judge against ...' (officium domini contra). The cases arose from
an information, presentment, denunciation, accusation or
inquisition. The largest single category were the presentments of
churchwardens. These presentments were founded upon lists of
articles, of the kind already quoted above, which were delivered to
churchwardens, who were sworn to make returns concerning the
questions asked. These returns by churchwardens were often called
the 'bill of detection'. We are told that the 'presentments could be
made upon proved or provable fact, upon a "fame" or rumour, or merely
upon "vehement suspicion". From the presentments were prepared
citations for persons accused to appear on a given court day at a
given time' (Brinkworth 1942:xi). All this was written down in the
main act book under the general heading which names the judge and
his authority, the place and date of the session, and usually the
parish. Often the presentments were written in advance before the
court met, usually four or five to a page, leaving some room for
further process.

Almost always the citations are now lost. These named the
judge, day and place of the court, the man cited and the offence
with which he was charged. This was addressed to the officiating
minister of the parish and had to be returned by him to the court
with a certificate stating when it had been served. The citations
were served on the minister by officials called 'apparitors'. If
these officials could not find the person named, the apparitor had
to certify on his oath that he had carefully searched for the party
and explain why he had failed to find him. The judge would then
order a citation 'by ways and means' (<u>viis et modis</u>) which the
apparitor had to serve personally if he could, otherwise by any
means available, for example by affixing it to the door of the
person's dwelling or the parish church. Again, the apparitor had to
certify as to what he had done.

When the accused appeared he took the oath <u>ex officio</u> 'the
oath which ecclesiastical authorities by virtue of their office
might administer to accused persons' (Brinkworth 1942:xi-xii). He
was then examined in open court in a trial before the judge;
witnesses might be called in. In complicated cases a series of
articles might be objected against the accused. Answers by the
accused, like the rest of this part of the trial, would be entered
in the act book. If there were sufficient grounds, the defendant
might be represented in the court by another. If the accused person
did not appear he was guilty of 'contumacy'. Having been called
three times by the court crier, he was pronounced contumacious and
either declared excommunicate or suspended immediately, or the
penalty was reserved until a specified later date. If he appeared
on the same day in person or by proxy he was absolved from
excommunication without any costs for contumacy, but had to pay a
fee to the apparitor. At the end of the court there would be a list
of excommunicated persons. A letter of excommunication was then
sent to the acting clergyman in the person's parish to be published
during divine service. The clergyman had to certify of having done
this on the letter of excommunication, which was returned to the

registry.

If a person appeared and accepted the charge, the next stage would be the penalty. If, however, he denied the fact and/or the 'fame', the accused might, before 1660 use 'purgation', that is the oaths of various neighbours, to prove his innocence. If he chose to do this, the judge would order him to purge himself with a specified number of honest neighbours, termed compurgators, on a set day.

> A proclamation giving notice that the purgation was to be made on such a day had to be given out in the parish church at least six days before. It called for all who had grounds for opposing the purgation and/or the compurgators to appear on a specified court day and bring forward their objections. If these objections were proved, the accused was pronounced guilty and penance was enjoined (Brinkworth 1942:xiv).

When the accused appeared at the court for purgation, he took an oath declaring his innocence. Then the compurgators also took an oath and declared that they believed that the accused was speaking the truth. The accused person was then declared innocent, restored to his good name and dismissed, often with a warning to avoid grounds for suspicion in the future. If the required number of compurgators did not appear or they refused to take the oath, he was declared to have failed and penance was ordered.

A person who had been excommunicated at an earlier stage for contumacy could be absolved by the judge after making a petition. He had to take an oath to obey the judge and was then restored to the sacraments. If the accused confessed his fault or failed purgation, penance was enjoined. The general form of the penance was the reading of a confession in a public or semi-public place. If it was completely public, it might be in the church before the whole congregation in time of service or in the market place. Sometimes the confession had to be read on successive occasions and in several places. A less public confession could be decreed before the minister, churchwardens and sometimes some extra parishioners. 'The details of penances varied considerably, but they included as

a rule a recitation of the details of the fault, an appeal for the
forgiveness of God and the offender's neighbours, and the joint
recitation by the penitent and congregation of the Lord's prayer'
(Brinkworth 1942:xiii). The details of the penance, including often
the fact that it was to be performed in penitential clothing, for
example in a white sheet, holding a white wand, were sent as
'schedules of penance or confession' addressed to the minister. They
were returned with a certificate of performance to the court. If
the penance was performed other than in church, it was usually
conducted by an apparitor who in turn had to certify as to its
performance.

In certain 'causes', upon the petition of the sentenced
person, the judge would allow the penance to be commuted into a
money payment. The sum and destination of the money, usually some
charitable cause, were fixed by the judge. These 'decrees of
commutation of penance' by the judge were filed in court and a copy
given to the petitioner. Throughout the process fees were extracted
for the work of the various officials and these, like much of the
proceedings, were noted in the act books. Sometimes a person was
excommunicated not because of the original offence, but because he
failed to pay the fees. This process may seem complex, requiring in
a full case with compurgators and a penance several court sessions
and numerous letters, certificates, schedules, etc. Yet it was
simplicity itself when compared to the plenary procedure, hence its
name 'summary' procedure. Dorothy Owen states that 'Summary
procedure could easily be upset by an ingenious lawyer and if the
prosecuting judge had any doubts about the outcome of a case he was
likly to submit it to the plenary procedure, which, though
lengthier, offered fewer opportunities for pleas of non-suit' (Owen
1970:39). Thus a number of 'mere office' cases joined the 'promoted
office' and instance cases which went through this other procedure.

The summary cases concerning Earls Colne have been
abstracted from the records of three jurisdictions. The
archdeaconry records are deposited at the Essex Record Office. They

consist of fifty-five 'Act' or correction and detection books
(D/ACA) for periods between 1540 and 1666: these are large bound
volumes, with an average of 400 pages per volume. There are
transcripts of some of the manuscripts by R.H. Browne and Dr A.
Clark (D/AZ/1,2). Many of the original documents are in an
extremely fragile condition. The documents were mostly written by
the clerk of the court both as a guide for action and as a record of
the proceedings. They are written in a mixture of English and Latin
with frequent abbreviations. As much of the detail was written in
court, it is often crowded and sometimes illegible.

There are similar difficulties with the summary records of
the bishop's two jurisdictions. The Consistory Court records are at
the Greater London Record Office at County Hall. There are
forty-three volumes of corrections and detections
(DL/C/300-29;614-26) which run from 1554 to 1671. The volumes are
again very large, leather bound volumes, of a similar form and
content.

The surviving records for the bishop's Commissary are in two
places. There are twelve volumes of acts (D/ABA) between 1616 and
1670 deposited at the Essex Record Office but only three cases from
Earls Colne were found in these. At the Guildhall Library there are
other volumes of Commissary ex officio acts (e.g. Ms. 9064, vols.
12-18, 1582-1629), but a search of a sample of these suggest that
almost all the cases came from in or near London and only one or
two Earls Colne cases might be found from a complete and laborious
search.

Records of plenary or instance jurisdiction
The records produced by this procedure are both briefer and less
informative than those produced by the summary procedure. This is
the result of the loss of records. We have seen that the act books
record most of the major stages and much of the information in
summary cases: only the detailed citations, schedules of penance
and decrees of commutation of penance are usually missing. With

plenary records, in Essex at least, the position is otherwise. What survives is the act book or journal of what happened. But, as already pointed out, this is 'little more than a record of "assignations" of the date and place of the next term, of the proctors acting in the suits, and of the fees due to the registrar' (Owen 1970:40). Often, it fails to give the parish, or any details about the accused; is written in very abbreviated Latin, and is clearly just a set of very brief abstracts from the process. What really went on is excellently summarized by Dorothy Owen and we cannot do better than repeat her summary of the procedure.

The general process follows the practice of common law. To paraphrase Owen's description (Owen 1970:40-1), the process begins with a written statement of the case - by the judge in promoted office cases, by the plaintiff in instance cases. In the 'contestation of suits', the accused either pleads guilty and is sentenced, or answers the accusation and the case proceeds. A 'term probatory' is assigned in which the prosecution should produce witnesses to prove the allegation, and a 'term to propound acts' is assigned for the prosecution to prove the validity of written statements made by its witnesses. Similar terms are assigned by the defendant to produce and verify counter claims. A 'term to conclude' is assigned. This is what is summarized in the assignation book. But behind it lies an even more complex reality. Dorothy Owen's full description of the system, although by her own admission 'much simplified', shows the complexities clearly enough. As she says, it was certainly a system that would produce very large quantities of records. Often the different kinds of papers were filed separately in bundles or registers; each diocese and archdeaconry filed its material in different ways. Many of the documents were wholly in Latin until 1733, although the depositions and some of the schedules of evidence and penance contained some vernacular.

To this general account of process we may add a few further points. Firstly, as regards witnesses in plenary proceedings, although 'the concurrent testimony of two witnesses was sufficient

in theory to settle most types of case in the ecclesiastical
courts. In practice it was usually necessary to produce more than
two witnesses ...' (Houlbrooke 1979:40-1). As regards sanctions to
enforce obedience, excommunication was not the only weapon. A
person might be either suspended or excommunicated. 'The suspended
man was forbidden to enter a church; the excommunicate was in
addition barred from the company of all Christians' (Houlbrooke
1979:48). In theory, if a person remained excommunicated for over
forty days, the bishop could apply for the royal writ de
excommunicato capiendo, which ordered the sheriff to imprison him.
Houlbrooke's evidence from sixteenth-century Norwich and
Winchester suggests that this happened only infrequently
(Houlbrooke 1979:50).

More generally, it is interesting to compare the procedure in
the church courts with other courts in the land. An overview is
presented by Geoffrey Elton who writes:

> Once a case had commenced, procedure was ... very like that
> used in the King's equity courts, which, in fact, had borrowed
> their methods from the Church courts. The parties exchanged
> written statements; proof was obtained by examining
> witnesses; and the stages of the process, as well as the final
> decision, were registered in act books. By contrast with the
> equity courts, those of the Church at all stages used oaths
> to bind the parties to future truthfulness and involved the
> judges far more as active pursuers of the facts ... (Elton
> 1969:103).

We may now look at the quantity and nature of surviving
records of plenary jurisdiction for courts which covered Earls
Colne. The records relating to plenary jurisdiction are again
spread in three depositories. The Archdeaconry of Colchester
records at the Essex Record Office consist of five volumes and two
files of depositions, that is the examinations and replies of
witnesses in plenary cases (D/ACD) at various periods between 1587
and 1641, as well as a mixed volume (D/AXD). The answers, usually to
interrogatories which are not included, are fairly legible and in

English after the first two volumes. The highly abbreviated recording of the process of cases is given in the 'Cause' books (D/ACC) which cover some of the years between 1588 and 1640. These are in Latin and give very little detail, often not even mentioning the parish or subject of the action. Only a summary of the cases which have been found relating to Earls Colne have been given; other cases could no doubt be found after further very time consuming searches.

The plenary records of the Consistory Court are voluminous and are deposited at County Hall, London. A search of two or three volumes from each of the major classes did not locate any Earls Colne cases. Though there are possibly cases, the fact that the parish is not given, and the highly abbreviated form of any information that does emerge, precluded a further search. The classes in which samples were taken were the personal responses to libels (DL/C/192-202), allegations (DL/C/142-71), examinations and replies (DL/C/205-73,628-34), assignation books (DL/C/87-108) and instance act books (DL/C/1-83,607-13). No doubt a patient search of the more than 200 volumes, each a large leather bound book of up to 700 pages, would reveal a few cases, and certainly for the social and ecclesiastical historian in general they are full of information.

The Commissary records are again split. There are eight volumes of 'Causes', that is abbreviated summaries of procedure, at the Essex Record Office (D/ABC) and eight volumes of 'depositions and cognate documents', that is mainly the examinations of witnesses (D/ABD). A search of all these revealed only two sets of depositions which involve Earls Colne inhabitants. There are many volumes of depositions, assignation books and miscellaneous cause papers of the Commissary Court at the Guildhall Library. A detailed search of these might reveal one or two Earls Colne cases, but sampling of a few volumes suggests that the return on the amount of labour required would be very small.

Church as registry: documents of record concerning testaments
A number of cases concerning testamentary business were heard
under the headings of summary or plenary proceedings, for they
involved disputes between persons. Furthermore, the record of wills
which were not witnessed, and 'nuncupative' wills, that is wills
which consisted of the wish of a dying testator on his death bed,
were also usually recorded in the ordinary court records. If a will
was not disputed the executors would exhibit the will, make oath as
to its validity, and obtain probate. This process was recorded in
the ordinary office act books, and later in special probate act
books. What happened then, and the various types of documents which
might appear, is well summarized by Dorothy Owen.

> The original will, with the sealed act of probate was
> attached or endorsed, was filed in court ... If an executor
> named in a will is unable or unwilling to undertake the
> labour he must formally renounce it by a renunciation,
> attested by a notary and filed in the court. When a person
> dies intestate, without having made a will, the ordinary
> deputes some person ... to administer his effects: such grants
> of administration were recorded in a separate journal
> register, or, at an earlier period, in the official's register
> of licences. Executors and administrators alike were
> required to execute bonds, the condition of which was
> faithful acounting and exhibition of an inventory of the
> goods of the deceased. If the ordinary required it, actual
> accounts of administrations were to be brought into court
> (Owen 1970:44-5).

Tuition bonds, for minors who were heirs of estates, were also to be
filed in court, but none of these survive for this period for the
Archdeaconry of Colchester. The inventories which seem to have been
kept separately have disappeared for most of Essex, but they were
clearly exhibited and the totals of inventories are given in the
act books for the periods 1575-1640 and 1663-1719.

Apart from a few loose wills in personal papers, the
surviving wills from Earls Colne are to be found in three
repositories. The wills of those who owned property in two counties

or two dioceses were proved at the Prerogative Court of Canterbury.
There are fifty-two surviving wills for Earls Colne from this
court. In certain cases, particularly where property was owned in
two or more archdeaconries, the will would be proved and survive at
the level of the bishopric. Voluminous probate materials survive
for the Commissary in Essex and Hertfordshire which are deposited
at the Guildhall. There are registers of wills, original wills,
bonds, probate act books and inventories. But a search of the
indexes and samples of the various classes revealed no Earls Colne
probate material. It is quite possible that a thorough search might
reveal one or two documents. There are also extensive probate
materials, both loose wills and registers, for the Consistory of
the Bishop of London, and seven Earls Colne wills have been found
among them. This series runs from 1507 onwards (DL/C/418ff,
DL/C/354ff County Hall). The vast majority of the wills for Earls
Colne were proved at the court of the Archdeacon of Colchester and
are hence found in either the sets of loose original wills or
registered copies at the Essex Record Office. There are some 325
wills either for inhabitants of Earls Colne, or people who left
bequests which mention Earls Colne (D/ACW, D/ACR).

It is possible to gain some impression of the survival of
those wills which were actually proved in the ecclesiastical court
in two further ways. Firstly, during the period 1567 to 1640 the
probate acts for some of the Essex wills are recorded in the
general act books and later, from 1663 onwards, in special probate
act books (D/ACAc). These volumes mention 184 wills as having been
brought to court and proved; of them, 171 have survived. Most of
those which are missing appear to have been pauper wills. A second
check is provided by the manor court rolls. According to customary
law, the property of the deceased held of the manor went to his heir
unless he left it by will to someone else. In order to do this he
had to surrender the property in the manor court 'to the use of his
will'. Thus part of certain wills refering to copyhold lands were
sometimes copied into the court rolls at subsequent transfers. Over

the period 1490 to 1750, of all the wills mentioned, there are some 71 wills which we have been unable to locate.

The wills themselves, as we have seen, were only a small part of the process of probate. Even though the inventories and accounts are missing, the probate acts and occasional testamentary disputes in the ecclesiastical courts give us further indication concerning what went on. For Earls Colne the two main classes are among the Archdeaconry of Colchester materials at the Essex Record Office. The probate and administrative acts whereby a will was formally proved survive from 1663 continuously through to 1750 (D/ACAc) and have all been searched: there are 107 for Earls Colne. The bonds to execute and administer wills have survived from 1678 onwards (D/ACWb) and there are 23 for Earls Colne up to 1750.

Church as registry: baptisms, marriages and burials
There are several theories as to why in 1538 Thomas Cromwell issued injunctions to every parish in England that a register of baptisms, marriages and burials be kept henceforth. J.C. Cox speculated that the original reason for such a move may have been financial, but that a proposed tax was dropped as a result of popular pressure (Cox 1910:1-2). Elton writes that 'the purpose, almost certainly, was to provide a statistical basis for government action, a record of the people of England...' (Elton 1969:111). The wording of the injunction merely states the method to be used:

> That you and every parson vicar or curate within this diocese shall for every church keep one book or register wherein you shall write the day and year of every wedding, christening and burying made within your parish for your time, and so every man succeeding you likewise. And shall there insert every person's name that shall be so wedded christened or buried ... Which book you shall every Sunday take forth and in the presence of the wardens or one of them write and record in the same all weddings, christenings and buryings made the whole week before ... And for every time that the same shall be omitted the party that shall be in the fault thereof shall forfeit to the church iiis iiid [3s. 3d.] to be employed on

the reparation of the same church ... (Cox 1910:2-3).
These injunctions were re-issued several times, but the main change
occurred when in 1597 a constitution of the clergy approved by the
Queen declared that registers were henceforth to be kept on
parchment, and parchment copies were to be made of those old
registers which were on paper, many of which were decaying rapidly.
It was further enacted, to prevent negligence or deceit, that 'the
whole of the entries of the previous week were to be read openly
and distinctly by the minister on Sunday, at the conclusion of
either mattins or evensong' (Cox 1910:6). It was also ordered that
the wardens should send a copy of the register each year to the
diocesan register where they were to be kept among the episcopal
archives. These 'Bishops Transcripts' seldom survive for an early
period, though many registers for English parishes have survived
from the middle of the sixteenth century or earlier. The only other
major change occurred in the middle of the seventeenth century.
After a number of years of destruction caused by the troubles of
the English Civil War and ejection of many ministers, it was
enacted in 1653 that ministers be required to give up their parish
register books to laymen who were to act for them. These new
officials were to enter all publications of banns, marriages,
births and burials. At the Restoration in 1660 the registers
reverted to the clergy.

The form and contents of parish registers in general is
fairly well known and straightforward. Many have been published by
local record and genealogical societies and good guides to their
contents and whereabouts have been provided. Their immense value
for demographic studies has meant that they have been more
carefully described and analysed than any other historical source.
Yet, even with their apparent simplicity, they 'pose some hidden
problems. They were kept very differently in different places -
with different degrees of precision and even on different
principles of selection' (Elton 1969:112). Distinctions between
birth and baptism dates, gaps in the registers, under-recording of

117

certain events at certain times, non-recording of religious nonconformists all need to be borne in mind.

The early Earls Colne parish registers are deposited at the Essex Record Office (D/P209/1/1-4) and consist of four parchment books running, with certain gaps, between 1558 and 1755. They follow the normal form of English parish registers in usually giving details concerning the names, dates and, in certain cases, parentage of those baptised, married and buried.

As well as the registers kept by the Anglican clergy, from the later seventeenth century onwards various nonconformist groups obtained the right to keep registers of births, marriages and burials. In Earls Colne the main documents of this kind are the registers of Quakers. These registers can be found at the Public Record Office (RG6) and the Library of the Society of Friends in London. Quaker registration of all kinds required considerable duplication involving two bodies: the Quarterly Meeting (which in the case of Earls Colne covered Essex) and the Monthly Meeting (which covered the Coggeshall area). The Quarterly Meeting register starts at 1668 and continues throughout the rest of our period although it becomes thin after the first quarter of the eighteenth century. The Monthly Meeting starts earlier in 1652. It should be noted that the years given in the microfiche start in January, not in March as in the originals.

The system of registration of births was to present duplicates to the registrar at the appropriate Monthly Meeting. There they would be scrutinized and signed; one copy would be given to the parents, the other, after being entered in the register, would be forwarded to the Quarterly Meeting where it would be registered again. The burials required duplicates to be registered at the Monthly Meeting where the burial ground was situated. If the deceased was not a member of that meeting, one copy would be sent for registration to the meeting to which he or she belonged, before being forwarded to the Quarterly Meeting for re-registration. Marriage, as in the Anglican register, was the most complicated. The parties concerned had first to appear before a Monthly Meeting and declare their intentions of marriage: this was similar to the Anglican publication of banns. Then they would be asked to prove that they were free of all others and had their parents' consent to marry. The parents themselves might be present, or they could send a letter showing that they gave their consent. The meeting would then appoint men to enquire fully into the man's 'clearness and sobriety of conversation', and women to look into the woman's 'clearness and orderliness'. These men and women would then have to report back to the next meeting. A certificate based on their findings would have to be produced at the second declaration - which was not necessarily at the same meeting house. Each time the parties signed the declaration. On the day of the marriage, duplicates were signed by the parties concerned and sent, if the marriage was held elsewhere, to the Monthly Meeting to which the woman belonged. There both copies would be scrutinized: one copy would be filed for preservation by the Monthly Meeting, the other copy forwarded to the Quarterly Meeting where it would also be filed. If the man belonged to a different meeting a notification in prescribed form would be sent to his Monthly Meeting for recording in the minutes.

Church as licensing authority

Throughout our period the Church exercised authority in the general areas of marriage, medicine and education. Among other things, this meant that all those who wished either to dispense with the normal forms of canon law marriage or to practise in the field of medicine or education, needed to receive a licence to do so. All these licences were primarily issued by the bishop, or on his behalf by his chancellor or official, often in the Consistory Court. It appears that similar registers might also be kept by the bishop's Commissaries in the archdeaconries of a large diocese such as London (Owen 1970:20). For Earls Colne, apart from a few presentments for unlicensed schoolmasters, midwives and surgeons in the normal ecclesiastical court records, the only aspect of this

licensing activity which has left any major trace is that in
relation to marriage.

A canon law marriage by the sixteenth century had to have
certain features. It must take place in the day time, in seasons
which were not prohibited, in the parish of the bride, between two
adults, and after the public announcement on three Sundays of the
public 'banns' which would give neighbours and others a chance to
put forward any objection to the marriage. If it was desired that
any of these conditions be broken, then it was necessary to obtain
a licence. The most frequently stated reason for obtaining a
licence seems to have been to avoid the open and demeaning
publicity of having one's name read out in church. By the later
seventeenth century in Earls Colne about half of the marriages were
by licence rather than banns. Although almost all of these were
also recorded in the parish register, the licences often include
extra details of occupation, residence and age which are of value
to the historian. It is clear that the licensing power of the
bishops goes back a long way, to at least the fourteenth century,
and that many such licences existed for earlier periods. For Essex
and Earls Colne, however, apart from a few scattered licences from
earlier periods, the bulk of licences have only survived from 1665
for the Bishop of London's Consistory (D/ALL), from 1681 for the
bishop's Commissary in Essex and Hertfordshire (D/ABL) and from
1681 for the Archdeacon of Colchester (D/ACL). At present it is not
clear why some people should have preferred one jurisdiction to
another, nor is it obvious that those who married by licence rather
than banns were different from the rest of the population even
though the Canons of 1603 had stated that 'no licence shall be
granted, but unto such persons only, as be of good state and
quality' (Burn 1788A:ii,426).

We have been speaking generally of 'licences', but in fact
most of the surviving Essex documents were not strictly speaking
licences at all. The codification arising from the Canons of 1603
led to the production of three types of document. There were the

120

licences themselves, of which only ninety-two have survived for
Essex (Emmison 1969:72). Then there were also 'allegations' and
'bonds'. It is possible to check the survival of such documents in
unusual detail since they overlap with the parish registers.
References to marriage by licence start to be recorded in the Earls
Colne parish register in 1683. Seven of the forty-seven marriages
between 1680 and 1699 are recorded as being by licence, but none of
these licences or the bonds and allegations that went with them
have been found. On the other hand, six bonds or allegations
referring to the attempts of Earls Colne inhabitants to marry in
other parishes have been found. During the period 1700 to 1714 only
three out of fifty-one recorded marriages in the parish register
mention a licence: none of these three have been found elsewhere.
The habit of marrying by licence clearly became more popular from
1715, for between then and 1750, of 223 recorded marriages, eighty
were stated to be by licence. All but three of these have left
traces in bonds or allegations. Simultaneously, eighty-two bonds or
allegations for Earls Colne inhabitants marrying elsewhere have
been found. One curious feature is the presence of a large number
of couples, some forty-eight in all, where neither partner is known
to be associated with Earls Colne. This may be connected to the
fact the vicar of Earls Colne from 1711 was Thomas Bernard, who was
a surrogate and empowered by the bishop to issue bonds, licences,
etc.

Church as poor law administrator
The gradual evolution of the Old Poor Law is summarized by Burn.

> Anciently, the maintenance of the poor was chiefly an
> ecclesiastical concern. A fourth part of the tithes in every
> parish was set apart for that purpose. The minister, under
> the bishop, had the principal direction in the disposal
> thereof, assisted by the churchwardens and other principal
> inhabitants. Hence naturally became established the
> parochial settlements (Burn 1788B:iii,5).

Later the monasteries shared in the relief of the poor, but with the abolition of the monasteries and confiscation of their lands, the State gradually became more involved in poor law administration. Various enactments of Henry VIII and Elizabeth which regularized the collection of a poor rate and instituted collectors and assessors of the poor rate to assist the churchwardens were summarized in the statute of 43 Eliz. c.2(1597) whereby it was enacted:

> The churchwardens of every parish, and four, three, or two substantial householders there, as shall be thought meet, having respect to the greatness of the parish, to be nominated yearly in Easter week, or within one month after Easter, under the hand and seal of two or more justices of the peace in the same county, ... shall be called overseers of the poor of the same parish (Burn 1788B:iii,307).

The prime duty of these officers was to collect a rate and then to disburse it to the poor. The method of raising this rate was stated in the same statute.

> 1. The churchwardens and overseers of the poor of every parish, or the greater part of them, shall raise weekly or otherwise (by taxation of every inhabitant, parson, vicar, and other, and of every occupier of lands, houses, ...) a convenient stock of flax, hemp, wool, thread, iron, and other ware and stuff, to set the poor on work - and also competent sums for the necessary relief of the lame, impotent, old, blind, and such other amount of them being poor as are not able to work, and also for the putting out poor children apprentices (Burn 1788B:iii,609).

Thus the major set of records produced are the accounts of the churchwardens and overseers of the poor which provide details of the amounts of poor rate collected and how it was expended. For some Essex villages these exist for periods in the sixteenth century and for many English parishes there are such records from the early seventeenth century. In Earls Colne, however, the records only survive from 1722. This book, with its varied contents, gives some idea of what has been lost (D/P209/8). It contains both the rates levied for the poor and some details of disbursements to the poor. This is supplemented from 1741 by the survival of the detailed accounts of the overseers (D/P209/12). There are no surviving churchwardens accounts before 1750.

Two overseers of the poor were chosen each year to collect the rate: one for each of the half yearly rates at Easter and Michaelmas. These rates give the amount, the occupier (who may be owner or tenant) and sometimes the place rated. Every rate had to be passed by two Justices of the Peace, who signed at the bottom of each rate listing. The earlier part of this book, before the start of the accounts in 1741, gives more detail on the disbursement of the rates, and also lists those in receipt of the standing collection. The accounts exist only for a very short time but contain important details about the lives of the poor in the workhouse, and as out pensioners. As well as collecting the rates and submitting them to the Justices and vestry, the overseers had to make a detailed account of their disbursements. Each account differs in the amount of detail the overseer thought necessary. Some, for instance, list exactly what each payment was, others just put 'to a bill' or 'to Joseph Pond' or whoever was owed the monies, and the amount paid.

One of the uses of the money collected by the overseers was to apprentice pauper children. The apprenticeship indentures created by this process sometimes survive and a collection for Earls Colne from 1681 exists (D/P209/14). There are fifty-two in all and they give the following details: the name of the child and sometimes his age, the parish officers and the name of the parish, the names of the consenting Justices, the name and occupation of the master or mistress, the date and the signatures of the parties concerned.

Apart from binding paupers' children, the overseers were responsible under the Justices for dealing with the maintenance of illegitimate children where there was some doubt as to whether their putative father would support them. Hence there was created a class of bonds in which the putative father, or another acting on his behalf, would bind himself under a large sum, to be responsible for the education and rearing of the illegitimately conceived infant. For Earls Colne there are some ten such bonds, starting in 1723 and ending in 1750 (D/P209/15/1). These bonds include: the names of the mother, the child (if known), the putative father, other bondsmen, the parish officers, the parish concerned, the presiding Justices, and also the penal value of the bond, the date and the signatures of the parties concerned.

It is clear that the basic premise of the system was that a parish was responsible for its poor. But who were its poor? With the huge geographical mobility of the whole period it was extremely difficult to decide where a person had legal 'settlement', in other words, where he should be sent to if he became destitute. This raised enormous complications and there is a vast legal and other literature on the subject. As Burn points out, the major settlement act of 1662 was one upon which 'there have been more cases adjudged, than upon any other act in the statute book' (Burn 1788B:iii,333). Burn summarizes the legal history of settlement as follows:

> By a statute made in the 12 R.2.c.7 (1388). The poor were to repair, in order to be maintained, to the places where they were born. By the 11 H.7.c.2 (1494) they were to repair to the place where they last dwelled, or were best known, or were born. By the 19 H.7.c.12 (1503) to where they were born, or made their last abode by the space of three years. By the 1 Ed.6.c.3 (1547) this was explained to be, where they had been most conversant by the space of three years. By the 1 J.c.7 (1604) they were to be sent to the place of their dwelling, if they had any; if not, to the place where they last dwelt by the space of one year; if that could not be known, then to the place of their birth. So that there were two kinds of settlement all along: by birth, and by inhabitancy, first for any indeterminate time, next for three years, then for one year. And this last continued to the time of the statute of the 13 & 14 C.2.c.12 (1662) which reduced the residence from the term of one year, to the space of forty days (Burn 1788B:iii,333).

This statute remained in force until after 1750. For Earls Colne, apart from references to settlement and removals in the parish

overseers' book, there are examinations (from 1726) and settlement
certificates. After 1697, these certificates permitted men and
women to move around by providing a guarantee that their own parish
would receive them back if they fell into poverty. For Earls Colne
there are 140 sets of such certificates of outsiders who arrived in
Earls Colne from 1677 to 1750. There are also 71 removal orders
from 1678 and disputes over removal, whereby the overseers of Earls
Colne or other parishes tried to rid themselves of needy persons.

Conclusions

We may wonder how much has been lost that was once recorded.
Further, we may speculate on how much still lies waiting to be used.
Naturally it is only possible to give very rough answers to these
questions. In general it should be stressed that record loss is
almost complete for the period up to 1540. We know that the courts
existed and the records were once there, but almost all have
disappeared. This gives a sense of a radical break, of the sudden
emergence of processes and ideas which in fact often date back to
at least the twelfth or thirteenth centuries. Even if we confine
our speculation to the period after 1540, we can only recover some
of the fragments of the past. If we look in semi-tabulated form at
the seven major roles of the Church, our impression in relation to
one parish is as follows.

1 Church as an administrative machine. Probably ninety per cent or
   more is lost, for the churchwardens' accounts and papers alone
   for the whole of the sixteenth and seventeenth centuries would
   have been very lengthy and a great deal else is lost.
2 Church as initiator of business; ex officio business. Although
   the survival is very good, at least half of the material, mainly
   that sent to the vicars and accused in the form of citations,
   schedules of penance, etc., is lost.
3 Church as a court for others. Here the loss of most of the cause
   papers in instance cases at the Archdeaconry Court means that we

only have a tiny proportion of what was written down, well under a quarter, in all probability.

4 Church as probate register. Although it is possible to check wills against other documents to show that most wills have survived, the loss of all the inventories, tuition and other bonds, and accounts, means that we still have less than half the material written at the time.

5 Church as register of baptisms, marriages and burials. Allowing for gaps in the registers and under-registration and nonconformity, we might estimate that roughly three-quarters of the births, marriages and burials that actually took place in the period between 1560 and 1750 were recorded.

6 Church as licensing authority. Well under half of the licences for the period after 1540 have survived.

7 Church as poor law administrator. The records here only survive for the last hundred years of our time span: the extensive records of poor administration for the sixteenth and seventeenth centuries have gone, leaving less than a quarter of what was created.

Thus what has survived is a fragment of what was once written about the inhabitants of England by the clerks of one of the major authorities.

Bibliography

Place of publication is London, unless otherwise specified.

Works referred to in the text

Anderson, John P. 1881. The Book of British Topography. Reprinted, Wakefield, 1976

Articles. 1635. Articles to be Enquired within the Arch-Deaconry of Colchester. Emmanuel College, Cambridge.

Bagley, J.J. 1971. Historical Interpretation. 2 vols.

Baker, J.H. 1979. An Introduction to English Legal History. 2nd edn.

Ballam, H. and Lewis, Roy. 1950. The Visitor's Book: England and the English as Others Have Seen Them: A.D. 1500 to 1950.

Bland, A.E., P.A. Brown and Tawney, R.H. 1919. English Economic History. Selected Documents.

Bloch, M. 1954. The Historian's Craft. Manchester.

Bradley, L. 1971. A Glossary for Local Population. Tawney House, Matlock, Derbyshire.

Brinkworth, E.R. (ed.). 1942. The Archdeacon's Court: Liber Actorum 1584. Oxfordshire Record Society. Vol. one.

    1943. 'The Study and Use of Archdeacons Court Records', Trans. Royal Hist. Soc., 4th ser., Vol. 25.

Britton, Edward. 1977. The Community of the Vill: A Study in the History of the Family and Village Life in Fourteenth-Century England. Toronto.

Bryson, W.H. 1975. The Equity Side of the Exchequer. Cambridge.

Burke, Thomas. 1942. Travel in England.

Burn, Richard. 1788A. Ecclesiastical Law. 5th edn, 4 vols.

    1788B. The Justice of the Peace, and Parish Officer. 16th edn, 4 vols.

Bibliography

Carrington, Dorothy. 1947. The Traveller's Eye.
Celoria, Francis. 1958. Local History.
Chamberlayne, John. 1737. The Present State of Great Britain.
    33rd edn.
Cheney, C.R. (ed.). 1970. Handbook of Dates for Students of English
    History.
Clanchy, M.T. 1979. From Memory to Written Record 1066-1307.
Clark, Peter. 1977. English Provincial Society from the Reformation
    to the Revolution.
Cockburn, James. 1975A. 'Early-Modern Assize Records as Historical
    Evidence', Journal of the Society of Archivists, Vol. 5, pp.
    215-31.
    1975B. Calendar of Assize Records: Sussex Indictments.
        Elizabeth I. First of six vols. also covering Herts., Essex,
        Kent and Surrey.
Coke, Edward. 1764. The Compleat Copyholder, republished in Three
    Law Tracts. First published in 1630.
Collinson, Patrick. 1967. The Elizabethan Puritan Movement.
Colt Hoare, Sir Richard. 1815. Catalogue of Books Relating to the
    History and Topography of England, Wales, Scotland, Ireland.
Cox, Edward G. 1949. A Reference Guide to the Literature of Travel.
    Vol. 3, England. Washington.
Cox, J. Charles. 1910. The Parish Registers of England.
Delaney, Paul. 1969. British Autobiography in the Seventeenth
    Century.
Dorson, Richard M. 1968A. The British Folklorists: A History.
    1968B. Peasant Customs and Savage Myths: Selections from the
        British Folklorists. 2 vols.
Elton, G.R. 1960. The Tudor Constitution: Documents and Commentary.
    Cambridge.
    1969. England 1200-1640.
Emmison, F.G. 1966. Archives and Local History.
    1969. Guide to the Essex Record Office. Chelmsford.
    1970-8. Elizabethan Life. 4 vols. Essex Record Office, County
        Hall, Chelmsford.
Emmison, F.G. and Gray, I. 1961. County Records. Historical
    Association.
Ewart Evans, G. 1960. The Horse in the Furrow.
    1970. Where Beards Wag All. The Relevance of the Oral Tradition.
    1975. The Days That We Have Seen.
    1976. From Mouths of Men.

Bibliography

Fisher, J.L. (ed.). 1946. Cartularium Prioratus de Colne. Colchester.

Gooder, E.A. 1961. Latin for Local History: An Introduction.

Goody, Jack (ed.). 1968. Literacy in Traditional Societies. Cambridge.

1977. Domestication of the Savage Mind. Cambridge.

Grieve, Hilda E.P. 1954. Examples of English Handwriting 1150-1750. Essex Record Office Publications, County Hall, Chelmsford.

Gross, Charles. 1897. Bibliography of British Municipal History. Reprinted 1966.

Guide. 1963. Guide to the Contents of the Public Record Office. Vol. 1.

Hale, Sir Matthew. 1971. History of the Common Law of England. Chicago. Reprint.

Hall, Hubert. 1920. A Repertory of British Archives.

Hanbury, H.G. 1944. English Courts of Law. Oxford.

Harley, J.B. with Phillips, C.W. 1964. The Historian's Guide to Ordnance Survey Maps. Published for the Standing Conference for Local History by the National Council of Social Service, 26 Bedford Square, London WC1.

Hastings, Margaret. 1971. The Court of Common Pleas. Connecticut. Reprint.

Hay, Denys. 1977. Annalists and Historians: Western Historiography from the Eighth to the Eighteenth century.

Hearnshaw, F.J.C. (ed.). 1905. Southampton Court Leet Records. Southampton Record Society. Vol. one.

Hector, L.C. 1958. The Handwriting of English Documents.

Hey, David G. 1974. An English Rural Community: Myddle Under the Tudors and Stuarts. Leicester.

Holdsworth, Sir W. 1966. A History of English Law. Volume one. 7th edn.

Hollingsworth, T.H. 1969. Historical Demography.

Hone, N.J. 1906. The Manor and Manorial Records.

Hoskins, W.G. 1957A. The Midland Peasant: The Economic and Social History of a Leicestershire Village.

1957B. The Making of the English Landscape.

1959. Local History in England.

1963. Provincial England; Essays in Social and Economic History.

1967. Fieldwork in Local History.

Houlbrooke, Ralph. 1979. Church Courts and the People during the English Reformation 1520-1570. Oxford.

Houston, Jane (ed.) 1972. Index of Cases in the Records of the Court

of Arches at Lambeth Palace Library 1660-1913. British Record
Society.
Hunnisett, R.F. 1961. The Medieval Coroner. Cambridge.
Jacob, Giles. 1741. The Complete Court-Keeper or Land-Steward's
Assistant. 4th edn.
1744. A New Law Dictionary. 5th edn.
Kuhlicke, F.W. and Emmison, F.G. (eds.). 1965. English Local History
Handlist. Historical Association.
Laslett, Peter. 1965. The World We Have Lost.
Latham, L.C. 1931. The Manor. Historical Association.
Latham, R.E. 1952. 'The Feet of Fines', Amateur Historian. Vol. 1,
no. 1.
1965. Revised Medieval Word-List: From British and Irish
Sources. Oxford.
Macfarlane, Alan. 1970. The Family Life of Ralph Josselin.
Cambridge.
(ed.). 1976. The Diary of Ralph Josselin 1616-1683. British
Academy, Oxford.
Macfarlane, Alan, Harrison, Sarah and Jardine, Charles. 1977.
Reconstructing Historical Communities. Cambridge.
and Harrison, Sarah. 1981. The Justice and the Mare's Ale: Law
and Disorder in Seventeenth Century England. Oxford.
Macfarlane, Alan et al. (eds.). 1980-1. Records of an English
Village; Earls Colne 1400-1750. Chadwyck-Healey
(Microfiche) Ltd, 20 Newmarket Road, Cambridge.
Maitland, F.W. (ed.). 1889. Select Pleas in Manorial and Other
Seignorial Courts. Selden Society, Vol. 2.
Maitland, F.W. 1911. Collected Papers, ed. H.A.L. Fisher. Vol. one.
1919. The Constitutional History of England. Cambridge.
Martin, C.T. 1910. The Record Interpreter. 2nd edn.
Massingham, H. and P. 1962. The Englishman Abroad.
Matthews, William. 1950. British Diaries. Cambridge.
1955. British Autobiographies. Berkeley.
Modus. 1510. Modus Tenendi Cur Baron Cum Visu Franci Plegii.
Reprinted 1915 by the Manorial Society. Also an edition of
1610.
Moir, Esther. 1964. The Discovery of Britain: The English Tourists
1540-1840.
Morant, P. 1816. The History and Antiquities of the County of Essex.
2 vols.
Mullins, E.L.C. 1958. Texts and Calendars: An Analytical Guide to

Bibliography

Serial Publications. Royal Historical Society.

Newcourt, Richard. 1710. Repertorium Ecclesiasticum Parochiale Londinense. 2 vols.

Notestein, W. 1938. English Folk: A Book of Characters.
1956. Four Worthies.

Order. 1650. The Order of Keeping a Court Leet and Court Baron. Reprinted 1914 by the Manorial Society.

Oschinsky, D. (ed.). 1971. Walter of Henley and Other Treatises on Estate Management and Accounting. Oxford.

Owen, Dorothy M. 1970. The Records of the Established Church in England. British Records Association.

Penney, Norman (ed.). 1920. The Household Account Book of Sarah Fell of Swarthmoor Hall. Cambridge.

Phythian-Adams, C. 1975. Local History and Folklore: A New Framework. Published for Standing Conference of Local History.
1979. Desolation of a City: Coventry and the Urban Crisis of the Late Middle Ages. Cambridge.

Pocock, J.G.A. 1957. The Ancient Constitution and the Feudal Law: A Study of English Historical Thought in the Seventeenth Century. Cambridge.

Pollock, Sir F. amd Maitland, F.W. 1968. The History of English Law. Cambridge. 2nd edn.

Ponsonby, Arthur. 1923. English Diaries.
1927. More English Diaries.

Powicke, F.M. (ed.). 1939. Handbook of British Chronology. Royal Historical Society.

Prothero, G.W. (ed.). 1894. Select Statutes and other Constitutional Documents Illustrative of the Reigns of Elizabeth and James I. Oxford.

Pugh, R.B. 1954. How to Write a Parish History.

Radcliff, G.R.Y. and Cross, G. 1954. The English Legal System. 3rd edn.

Ravensdale, J.R. 1974. Liable to Floods: Village Landscape on the Edge of the Fens A.D. 450-1850. Cambridge.

Razi, Zvi. 1980. Life, Marriage and Death in a Medieval Parish. Cambridge.

Redstone, L.J. and Steer, F.W. 1953. Local Records: Their Nature and Care.

Rogers, Alan. 1977. Approaches to Local History. 2nd edn; first titled This Was Their World.

Rogers, J.E. Thorold. 1909. The Economic Interpretation of History. 7th edn.

Roll. 1434. Roll Recording Forms of Precedents in Various Manors. Birmingham Public Library (Ref. 383854).

Rye, Walter. 1888. Records and Record Searching: A Guide to the Genealogist and Topographer.

Rye, William B. 1865. England as Seen by Foreigners in the Days of Elizabeth and James the First. Reprinted New York, 1967.

St Clare Byrne, M. (ed.). 1981. The Lisle Letters. 6 vols. Chicago.

Sims, Richard. 1856. A Manual for the Genealogist, Topographer, Antiquary and Legal Professor.

Smith, Harold. no date. The Ecclesiastical History of Essex. Colchester.

Somerville, R. 1951. Handlist of Record Publications. British Records Association.

Spufford, Margaret. 1974. Contrasting Communities: English Villagers in the Sixteenth and Seventeenth Centuries. Cambridge.

Stephens, W.B. 1973. Sources for English Local History. Manchester. New enlarged edition, Cambridge, 1981, which omits transcripts of documents.

Stubbs, William. 1870. Select Charters and Other Illustrations of English Constitutional History. Oxford.

Tanner, J.R. 1940. Tudor Constitutional Documents A.D. 1485-1603. Cambridge.

Tate, W.E. 1946. The Parish Chest: A Study of the Records of Parochial Administration in England. 3rd printing, 1960. Cambridge.

Tawney, R.H. and Power, E.E. (eds.). 1924. Tudor Economic Documents. 3 vols.

Thirsk, J. and Cooper, J. (eds.). 1972. Seventeenth Century Economic Documents. Oxford.

Thompson, Paul. 1978. The Voice of the Past: Oral History. Oxford.

Thoyts, E.E. 1893. How to Decipher and Study Old Documents.

Upcott, William. 1818. A Bibliographical Account of the Principal Works Relating to English Topography. 3 vols. Reprinted Wakefield, 1978.

Vansina, Jan. 1973. Oral Tradition: A Study in Historical Methodology. Translated by H.M. Wright.

Webb, Sidney and Beatrice. 1908 on. English Local Government. 5 vols.

West, John. 1962. Village Records.

Bibliography

Williams, C.H. (ed.). 1967. English Historical Documents, Vol. 5,
    1485-1558.
Wilson, Francesca M. 1955. Strange Island: Britain through Foreign
    Eyes 1395-1940.
Wrightson, Keith and Levine, David. 1979. Poverty and Piety in an
    English Village: Terling 1525-1700.
Wrigley, E.A. (ed.). 1966. An Introduction to English Historical
    Demography.

Supplementary reading

State records
Barnes, T.G. Somerset 1625-1640.
Cockburn, J.S. (ed.). Crime in England 1550-1800.
Dibben, Alan. 1968. Title Deeds: 13-19th Centuries. Historical
    Association.
Foster, C.W. (ed.). 1920. 'Final Concords of the County of Lincoln',
    vol. 2. Lincs. Rec. Soc., vol. 17. Introduction.
Galbraith, V.H. 1934. An Introduction to the Use of the Public
    Records. Oxford.
Jones, W.J. 1967. The Elizabethan Court of Chancery. Oxford.
Trotter, E. 1919. Seventeenth Century Life in the Country Parish.

Estate records
Davenport, F.G. 1906. The Economic Development of a Norfolk Manor
    1086-1565.
Newton, K.C. 1910. The Manor of Writtle.
Simpson, A.W.B. 1960. An Introduction to the History of the Land Law.
    Oxford.
Thirsk, Joan (ed.). 1967. The Agrarian History of England and Wales,
    vol. 4, 1500-1640. Cambridge.
Wilkerson, J.C. (ed.). 1974. 'John Norden's Survey of Barley, Herts.
    1593-1603', Cambs. Antiquarian Record Society. Publication of
    a map with a detailed survey.

Church records
Camp, A.J. 1963. Wills and their Whereabouts.
Hill, Christopher. 1963. Economic Problems of the Church. Oxford.
Marchant, Ronald A. 1969. The Church under the Law: Justice
    Administration and Discipline in the Diocese of York
    1560-1640. Cambridge.

Bibliography

Peters, Robert. Oculus Episcopi; Administration in the Archdeaconry
    of St Albans 1580-1625. Manchester.
Purvis, J.S. 1953. An Introduction to Ecclesiastical Records.
Steel, D.J. (ed.). 1968. National Index of Parish Registers. 2 vols.
Swinburne, Henry. A Treatise of Testaments and Last Wills. Various
    editions.